Praise for

Resumes are Worthless

by Dale Callahan

"Dr. Callahan's book – *Resumes are Worthless* - is an utterly fascinating read with more interesting material on how to build a career and financial independence than I have ever read. Callahan truly captures the essence of what is required to be an asset to our society all while providing for the person performing the work. This is not your typical book written around trendy management principles, self-serving egocentric methods or abstract career goals but rather a precise guide to connecting with your passion and building a long lasting and enjoyable career."

-- Timothy Taylor - author of
Launch Fever
An entrepreneur's journey into the
secrets of launching rockets,
a new business and living a happier life

"A timely book. Dale Callahan gives you a proven strategy for success in our 'new normal' world. *Resumes are Worthless* will fundamentally change the way you view your job."

-- Don Appleby, Technology Consultant and Educator,
www.profappleby.com

"Everyone has to read Dr Callahan's book *Resumes are Worthless*! For the first time you can actually connect the YOU that you want to be to the career you WANT to have. Expect to be surprised with all the practical information that we all need to see to help us with where we really want to go!"

-- Denise Jeffries
SVP, Dir Data Warehouse
BBVA Compass

"Like it or not, admit it or not, the business world changed and it's not going back. *Resumes are Worthless* is a critical guide to this new world, not only for professional success but for finding happiness and fulfillment in your work (and life)."

-- Glenn S. Phillips
Consultant and Author of *Nerd-to-English*

"*Resumes are Worthless* is a powerful and dynamic must read for the wandering soul dying to find a way out of the corporate wasteland. Dale reveals the secrets that can change your rat race existence to a passion filled life!"

-- Russell T. Hyde, P.E.
Hyde Engineering
158 Business Center Drive
Birmingham, Alabama
205.982.0900
rusty@hyde-egr.com

"My name is Brian Rabon and I am a Company Of One... It all started when I met Dale back in 2004. I was at a point in my life when I was caught up in the corporate rat race. Dale made me question why I kept getting up every day and working for someone else. His teachings rekindled the entrepreneurial fire in me, which had always been burning but afraid to really shine. Today I am the president of my own company, The Braintrust Consulting Group, I am following my heart and above all I am enjoying the new found freedom I have create for myself. It hasn't been easy, in fact it has been the hardest thing I have ever done. I have faced fears that I didn't know that I could have. Fortunately for me Dale has been there every step of the way guiding me, find his wisdom for yourself; read, study, and live the practices described in *Resumes are Worthless* and you will be well on your way to truly living. "

-- Brian M. Rabon, CSP, PMP
President
The Braintrust Consulting Group
www.yourpmpartner.com

"The ideas Dale covers in his book are phenomenal. They will not let you stand still – they will challenge you to take action – and take control. I found the greatest challenge and opportunity by getting outside my comfort zone. I didn't realize what was set into motion when I got outside the box I had let others create for me. I didn't know and it was kind of scary. But I knew I could be doing more; more for myself, more for my family, and more for the community if I would step out and create my calling. It is hard work and requires ownership of your actions, but that is the most fulfilling aspect of it all. I have traded all the old excuses for responsibly and action, because I am a company of one."

-- Frank Flow
Employee Benefit Specialist
Northwestern Benefits,
a subsidiary of Northwestern Mutual

RESUMES ARE

WORTHLESS

How to Find the Work You Love and Succeed.

Dale Callahan, Ph.D., P.E.

Published by ADC Publishing

Edited by Kathryn Marion

Cover design by Catrina Callahan

Printed in the United States of America

ISBN-13: 978-1456496432

First Edition

Printing ADC-12301000100

This publication is designed to provide accurate and authoritative information with regard to the subject matter covered. It is provided with the understanding that the publisher is not engaged in rendering legal, accounting, or other professional advice. If legal advice or other expert professional assistance is required, the services of a competent professional person should be sought.

To my lovely wife Lea,

to my family,

and to the clients, alumni, and staff of IEM!

To God be the Glory!

CONTENTS

About the Author...iii

How to use this book...v

What to expect from this book...vii

1 Voted off the Island...1

2 Taught to be Average?..7

3 Six Actions that Lead to Success...21

- Action 1 Successful people are not victims; they take responsibility for their lives...23

- Action 2 Successful people have passion...................................27

- Action 3 Successful people have vision....................................30

- Action 4 Successful People Take Risks....................................32

- Action 5 Successful people set goals.......................................34

- Action 6 Successful people EXECUTE.......................................37

4 Your Company of One..41

5 Managing Your Company of One...........................57

6 COO for your Company of One.............................61

7 CFO for your Company of One..............................71

8 CRO for your Company of One..............................81

9 CMO for your Company of One.............................91

10 CEO for your Company of One............................109

11 Networking for Introverts.................................127

- Networking 101..133

- Networking 102..140

- Networking 103..142

- Networking 201 The Reverse Interview.................144

Appendix - An Example of Joe's calling..................149

Afterword...155

Recommended Resources.......................................157

More from Dale Callahan..163

References..165

ABOUT THE AUTHOR

Dale Callahan is a professional speaker, trainer, and consultant in addition to acting as Director of the Executive Graduate program in Information Engineering and Management (www.uab.edu/iem) at the University of Alabama at Birmingham (UAB). In addition, Dale is the founder of AskDrCallahan Homeschool Solutions (AskDrCallahan.com).

Before getting trapped in corporate America, Dale was the founder and/or co-founder of several businesses. Since escaping his entrapment at BellSouth, he has founded or co-founded other businesses in wireless technology, real estate, and internet marketing.

In 2000, Dale took on a role he initially refused on more than one occasion: running the professional graduate program in Information Engineering and Management (IEM) at UAB. There, Dale has worked with professionals in companies such as Wachovia Bank, AT&T, Blue Cross Blue Shield, Compass Bank, US Steel, Honda, Mercedes, Regions Bank, Southern Company, KB&R, Norwegian Cruise Lines, various federal and state government agencies, and many others. Dale has consulted and coached professionals to hone their careers into something they *want*, not just what they think they can get.

Dale lives in Birmingham, Alabama, with his wife and three of his children. His oldest daughter, son-in-law, and grandson live in the same city. Dale shares his thoughts on entrepreneurship and taking control of your career in his blog at DaleCallahan.com.

HOW TO USE THIS BOOK

I tend to read books in bizarre ways—sometimes even back to front. When I get a book, I want to quickly learn if it is worth my time and then determine how I can best get the gems of information out of it in the shortest time. Sometimes I scan entire books in minutes—other times, however, the authors force me to think, so it takes much longer.

In my opinion, the critical part of any book is in the questions the author asks. The book you are holding will show you the "big picture" (the strategic view) of your career in a way you have probably never considered. The truths you find here

The questions are not magical, but your answers might be!

should open your eyes and push you to think of your career in a whole new light—and they will put you back in control.

Yet, once you get past this first step, you have work to do, because from that point, I only ask questions—and the answers are up to you. Trust me, I have taught this material dozens of times, and the people who truly make it happen have taken the time to think about their strategic view and answer the questions. *The questions are not magical, but your answers might be!*

The first chapter is about seeing the problem clearly. As an engineer, I know you cannot solve any problem without clearly identifying it. So first, we will look at the realities of the problem of work and career—it is a hard and sober look, but a necessary one. Then, we will begin to look at the strategies that really work, and discover what makes some people succeed at work while many just sit by and become average.

Enjoy your reading and thinking, but take note: *the thinking is more important than the reading!* So be prepared to think your way through this. After all, the thinking is all about *you*—your career and your ability to make money.

And for updates and new resources, be sure to visit

Resumesareworthless.com.

WHAT TO EXPECT FROM THIS BOOK

Note: This book was originally titled "Company of One", but market testing resulted in a new title of "Resumes are Worthless." But, titles aside, you will truly see that you are a "company of one" and that "resumes are <u>worthless</u>"!

I wrote this book because I found many great authors who have alluded to the concept of a Company of One, but none I have seen have delved into the subject to peel back the layers of the onion to see what is underneath.

I love material like this. It inspires me, and I hope it inspires you, too. Here are some of the results you can expect from this book:

- You will start thinking differently about your work, your co-workers, and your employers;
- You will become positive and think about things as opportunities instead of problems;
- You will become more confident because you will know you have many more options than you once thought;
- Your employers and customers will begin to see you as a more valuable asset than ever before;
- You will meet many people who can truly have a positive impact on your ability to make a living;
- You will start to see opportunities everywhere you look.

But all of these personal benefits do not come from me—they will come from *you*! First, you have to do the work. So let's get started.

1

VOTED OFF THE ISLAND

"It's just a job. Grass grows, birds fly, waves pound the sand. I beat people up." Muhammad Ali [1]

My corporate career started immediately after engineering school. While in college, I had participated in a co-op program working with a large telecom company. Once out of school with a fresh new degree, I took a job with the same company. I was excited and ready to conquer the world, and to be paid well to do it.

But, I did not take the job based on a thought-out career strategy or job search. Instead, the job I would use to break in my new degree came from a chance meeting at a mailbox. The manager of the telecom company lived across the street. One day when we

> *The first five years on this job were a corporate nightmare. I walked out of the excitement of an engineering degree from a top engineering school straight into a Dilbert cartoon.*

both were checking our mail, he told me that I should work for them. After all, he said, they needed "new blood" in the company and were actively recruiting. So I went to work.

The first five years of this job was a corporate nightmare. I walked out of the excitement of an engineering degree from a top engineering school straight into a Dilbert cartoon. I was working for BellSouth in a networking control center responsible for a particular geographical region. Instead of creating things and 'doing engineering,' I was pushing paper and sitting in meetings where we measured seemingly insignificant details of the work of others. And, of course, we were graded on how well those in our region performed.

After five years, I still struggled to understand how those crazy things we measured indicated customer satisfaction and network performance. On top of simply being bored, I was in a constant battle to treat my people the right way even though management wanted them to be slaves. I constantly took heat from the bosses.

Most of my employees were women, and several were divorced single mothers. After dropping their children off at school, they would make a quick breakfast in the breakroom and eat at their desks. One day my boss walked in to get coffee (something he did several times every morning) and stopped at my desk to ask, "How much work do you think your people are getting done eating at their desk?"

I replied, "as much as you are getting done walking back and forth to the coffee pot." Needless to say, I was not on the management fast track—besides, the work was boring, the management oppressive, and the morale negative.

CASPER APPEARS

The control center I was working in was just a monitoring point. When things broke, we were responsible for coordinating the work of many other people on other floors and in other buildings to get the problem resolved and customer service restored. Being ADD (Attention Deficit

Disorder, as diagnosed by those around me) and not wanting to just sit and wait, I had a tendency to go to the point of trouble to see if I could get the real scoop about what was happening. Even as an introvert, I preferred to get the facts from the people who were doing the work—all union member employees. Once the union "craft" employees realized the college kid was not a know-it-all (which I could not have faked if I wanted to), they thought I could be trusted. As a result, I got the real story and quality information—and often better and faster results to boot.

However, my being out of my office got me nicknamed "Casper." The end result is that I often got into a mess with management for being away from my desk. My manager would ask my staff, "Where is Dale?" and they would simply shrug their shoulders. The manager would then see the broken chains where I had slipped away. My role as Casper is just one example of me "not fitting in." Needless to say, my management reviews did not go well.

'GOING POSTAL'

After a short time on the job, I was suffering from disillusionment, anger, depression, and many other ailments, both mental and physical. I knew only one thing: something was wrong. I tried to do all the right things to "work hard and prosper." Yet, when I looked around me, I saw people who worked harder and longer than I had, who had more experience than I did, and yet seemed to have no more prosperity nor enjoyment of their work than I was having.

I wondered why they had continued year after year working at a job and a company where they did not seem happy. Their reasons were plenty, but they basically came down to three statements:

- "I am too committed to leave." (Which translates into "I am too close to retirement now.")
- "I am vested now and would lose too much." (I did not even know what 'vested' meant until much later in my career.)
- "We make too much money; others will not pay as much. And our benefits are also too good."

Of course, the only solution they had to offer was to "hold your nose and do your job" for 30 years, then take the retirement package. I soon began to understand all too well what was meant by "going postal," yet I refused to give in to the idea of "this is just how things work."

I played the rebel, tried to make things 'right,' and tried to treat my people well. Of course, playing the rebel is never a comfortable position—I guess I just loved the misery. If I had any talent in art, I would have been drawing my own Dilbert cartoons.

For about eight more years, I survived in this chaos. Some things did seem to get marginally better, yet I am not sure if they really got better or if I just got better at dealing with the system or if I simply felt better as a result of my corporate lobotomy.

LET'S PLAY BALL

One thing being a rebel can do is label you as "not a team player." My not being a team player was set in stone with a wonderful event I have yet to live down—so I might as well tell you about it. I was in a group which had experienced a wonderful leader, followed by several bureaucrats. I pretty much ignored it all and got the job done. But a new manager came on the scene—one that wanted to create a true rock-star team. He called us into a meeting to tell us that he wanted us to behave like the team in the movie *Apollo 13*—coming together to get amazing things done against the odds.

I admired his enthusiasm for the job—as long as I was left alone to do mine. So in a "team-building meeting" he pulled us together to play a game where we were to pass a ball between each other as fast as possible. The rule was that we all had to touch the ball, passing it from the first person to the last as fast as possible. (Have you played this "team-building game"?)

I got up and walked out. The manager was devastated—his team was DOA (dead on arrival). His allusions of being a grand leader with the Apollo 13 team were crushed in a single rebellious moment. He talked to me later that day and I was pretty hard on him. Not long after, he decided that he did not want to manage people anymore and went back to a staff role. On the good side, we both lived through it, and he and I are now friends (we just don't play ball together).

VOTED OFF THE ISLAND

But, just as I thought I had some things figured out and had learned 'the game', I was voted "least likely to succeed" in my group during a corporate downsizing move. Actually, the term they used was "at-risk", but the reality is that the managers voted me off the island, saying I was not a team player. Who could have seen that coming?

So, suddenly, I was out of a job. The next few months resulted in a mixture of depression and elation. I was devastated by the loss and the rejection—kind of the feeling you get when your high school girlfriend dumps you. For the first time in years, I felt free, but free to do what, I did not know.

It was nothing a little Prozac couldn't control. I starting thinking about the people I had worked around—including those who voted me off the island. I started to feel sorry for them—realizing that while I was afloat in the sea, I just might find another island, but they likely never would. In fact, at the time I am writing this, none of them has left except those who retired or were downsized.

The main thing I discovered, though, was a world of opportunity. I found people who love—really love—what they do. It was bizarre! I had heard about these creatures who loved their work, but never had seen one in person. I discovered people living the dream—not as bums on the beach (I have met them also), but people who seem to have discovered the true American dream.

I wanted to play their game!

DEVELOP YOUR COMPANY OF ONE

"For you to achieve any kind of success, execution is everything."
Brian Tracy in Eat That Frog! [2]

- Write down your "To Do" list for the next week. Nothing fancy; just write out what you plan to do next week. (If you are a list-maker, this is easy; if not, try it anyway.)

  For example (in case you are not a list maker) I might write:

  - Mow the grass
  - Turn in budget for next year
  - Look at buying a new computer
  - Look over meeting notes from last staff meeting
  - Prepare for weekly staff meeting
  - Clean out my email
  - Clean out my inbox at work

- Write down your frustration with your current employer or boss(es). These can be personal concerns or business issues:
  - What are they doing wrong?
  - How are they missing the objectives of the business?
  - How are they serving their customers?
  - How do they treat you?
  - Do they inspire you to do more or do they push you to the "postal" side?

Write these down. Nothing elaborate is needed, but we *will* refer back to them later.

2

TAUGHT TO BE AVERAGE?

"Great teachers are wonderful. They change lives. We need them. The problem is that most schools don't like great teachers. They're organized to stamp them out, bore them, bureaucratize them, and make them average." Seth Godin [1]

A key to finding solutions to problems is to first clearly understand the problem. Your career and work life are no exceptions. If you are not completely thrilled with your career, then you probably wonder if another job, or another company, will be any different. After all, it seems many people are not happy with their work. In this chapter, we will explore some assumptions as well as the realities of your situation.

WARNING: The material in this chapter is a solemn look at the situation. You need to understand it, but do not go out to invest in Prozac as you read this. If you are already on Prozac, make sure you have taken today's dosage before reading on. If you do not want to deal with the problem, skip ahead to the next chapter where we begin to look at the solution.

A REALITY CHECK FOR COLLEGE GRADUATES

I teach in an engineering school, but since most of my work is with professional graduate clients (we call our "students" clients since that is the real relationship we have with them) I see very few undergrads. But, in the two courses per year I do teach to undergraduates, those students are all seniors ready to go to work.

The subjects I teach (wireless communications and networking protocols, if you care to know) are not really going to be key to most of their careers. Yet, knowing we do *not* teach our undergrads how to succeed in industry, I try to take some time in my class to teach them what really matters.

Ok, some engineering faculty do teach their students skills to apply on the job. But we do not teach them *how* to get a job, and we do not teach them the realities of the job. Here are some points I give them about how their life will be five years post-graduation. I call it "Five Years: The Good, the Bad, and the Ugly."

THE GOOD:

In five years, most of you will be:

- working in a management role,
- working on teams with other disciplines,
- using skills and technologies you have not heard of to date,
- living in a nice house, and
- in the solid middle class looking like you are doing very well.

THE BAD:

In five years, most of you will:

- be looking for another job,
- have been fired (called by many names such as 'downsized') at least once, and
- have a negative outlook toward your job and company.

THE UGLY:

In five years, most of YOU will be:

- worried about making ends meet,
- in serious financial debt,
- suffering from a physical ailment related to stress, and
- feeling trapped.

After I cover this Good/Bad/Ugly part of my presentation (and I do go on to show them hope), I find some of them doubt me, but most seem to be worried about how accurate I might be. I assure them that, after having experienced it personally and having taught and coached hundreds of others, I am sure this is very accurate.

How about you? How many of those Good/Bad/Ugly points directly relate to *your* life? How did you get here?

EDUCATION AT WORK

Twelve years of school. This is where most of us really start our careers. In *theory*, those twelve years of basic education prepare us for the world of work. But in *reality*, all it does is prepare us for college—for yet another four, or more, years of education. Then college is meant to prepare us for the world of work. But what is *really* being taught?

Remember when your parents were so proud of you as you advanced from one grade to another in school? Perhaps you are expressing that same pride now with your children. Yet, I remember thinking, "Mom, all

> Every year, I was moved along with the masses like cattle being herded in the great system of education. I do not think I did anything stellar. I just followed directions.

I did was what they told me to." Every year, I was moved along with the masses like cattle being herded in the great system of education. I do not think I did anything stellar. I just followed directions.

Personally, I hated school. I remember trying to skip school in first grade. It was a total bore from beginning to end. I was thrilled when I got to college and was no longer held prisoner every day.

But, even in college I noticed that I did not have to think; I only had to learn how to follow yet another set of instructions. I showed up to class, got the syllabus (the rules of the class), studied the material (OK, studied might be too strong a word), took the tests, and, at the pre-assigned time, the term was over and I got a grade. From Day One of my engineering studies, I pretty much knew the rules all the way through, so I followed the yellow brick road right to the stage where the president of the university handed me my empty diploma holder.

Looking back, I can see that, all along the way from first grade to the end of my college days, I was receiving thought control. I was being taught to follow instructions, conform to the group, and respect authority. And, of course, I was being taught how to view the world, how to view government, how to view school, even how to view myself. In the end, they were telling me how to get along in the world of work. The education system was designed well to produce workers for the American corporate system.

GET A DEGREE AND GET A GOOD JOB

The fact is that in both K-thru-12 schools as well as in colleges (or other institution of advanced education) we are told how the world works and how we are to work in the world in order to succeed. The end goal of it all is a job. OK, sometimes we call it a 'career,' but let's be clear: they (the teachers and those who in their infinite wisdom counsel you whether you ask for it or not) always talk in terms of jobs and going to work.

The high-school and college years are particularly troubling in that you are constantly being groomed for work—but work for whom? To what end? To get a good paying job, of course!

SUCCESS?

Yes, this educational system is thought of as the modern path to success. But zoom out and take a bigger look. You are born, grow, attend twelve years of school, attend four years of college, perform a mission in a career (usually someone else's mission), work at it for thirty years, and then retire.

Yes, I have just described what many people believe and sell as the American Dream. This is what most of our parents have told us ... "get a good job, work hard, and live the good life." Or, to put another way, here is the equation we have been sold:

12 yrs of school + 4 yrs of college + 30 yrs of work

= Happy Retirement

HOUSTON, WE'VE HAD A PROBLEM

I think most of us realize that this system of doing things is broken. Careers no longer last thirty years. Jobs are not secure. Holding a degree does not even mean you are guaranteed a job! And think about it: you go through all of this work and education so you might end up being...average. In fact, that is what we are trained to be: average. *Who wants to be average?*

You might be thinking, "I know! This is nothing new to me." Then you understand the problem: the formula is flawed. Yet, we continue to march to the orders given to us by drummers over the years, and we are, in turn, handing our children over to the same set of drummers. Worse yet, *we have become the drummers!*

But do you really see all the impacts of the system? Consider these quotes related to this version of the American Dream. Which do you believe?

- In a survey of 5,000 people by the Conference Board in January 2010, only 45% of those surveyed said they were satisfied with their jobs, down from previous years.[2]

- A 2007 Gallop Poll indicated 77% of people *hate* their jobs.[3]

- Another survey says 87% of Americans 'dislike' their jobs.[4]

Frankly, I am not sure which is right, but clearly a lot of people are *not* satisfied with their jobs. Most troubling to me is that this data comes from people working in the USA—the freest nation in the world! People here have every choice and every opportunity, yet a majority of them are not happy. In fact, in the freest nation in the world, many people feel enslaved in their jobs.

STRESS

Now consider that our jobs might be impacting our health:

- "...workers suffer a significant increase in blood pressure as they return to the office after the weekend."[5]

- Research published several years ago in the *British Medical Journal* showed a 20-percent spike in heart attacks at the beginning of the week.[6]

- According to the Centers for Disease Control (CDC), up to 90% of doctor visits in the US could be stress-related illnesses.[7]

- About 43% of American families spend more than they earn each year[8] and 41% live paycheck to paycheck[9].

- The average worker who works 40 hours per week (yeah, right), and does so for thirty years or more, spends at least 60,000 hours of their life at work. This does not include commuting, overtime, and thinking about work.

- Even when they are away from work, the typical American spends time thinking about working—often dreading going back to work or complaining to others about their work. I do not have a statistic about this, but if you do not believe me, just go to lunch with co-workers. What do they talk about during their time away from the office?

- The average American spends more than half of their "awake" time at work. Add the commute, some overtime or after-work issues, and you have little time for yourself or your family.

If we are really living the American Dream, then, for a great many people, the dream has become a nightmare. The average American is NOT living the American dream at all. They are not happy and not healthy. They dread getting up in the morning and going to work. They live for Friday, love Saturday, and are depressed on Sunday because they dread Monday. They have children that they dearly wanted, yet they rarely have time for those children beyond feeding them—and much of that is done at a fast-food drive-through window.

> If we are really living the American dream, then, for a great many people, the dream has become a nightmare.

THE TARGET HAS MOVED

Now, in case you think I am down on the educational system and all the advice we got from Mom and Dad, we need to realize that our economy is dynamic. The system worked for our parents' generation—it was not perfect, but it worked.

But things have changed. Hard work and integrity are still key, but what the economy offered to our parents and grandparents is very different than what it offers us today. The twentieth century was wild with the advent of both the industrial and the information revolutions. People moved away from the farm and from working for themselves in a massive way.

DID YOU KNOW. . .

That the idea of retirement is a new concept in our society? This revolutionary, twentieth-century idea offered great hope to Americans and became a major part of the American Dream. Yet, ironically, the ever-increasing costs of retirement plans are one of the things killing the American corporation that our parents and grandparents loved.

Of course, people have been moving into cities since the beginning of civilization, but in the 1900s, massive changes in our economy were centered on goods and services in cities. The concept of a job was really hammered into a standard with the need for huge numbers of people to work on processes, usually in factories. The standard workday also became important, creating a hard 8-to-5 mentality in our society. Companies hired for the long term, and many people did, in fact, have solid thirty-year runs concluding with an attractive retirement package.

What has happened is that the economy has changed and companies have had to change to survive.

- Customers are savvy, are better informed, and have more options than ever before.

- The Internet provides a worldwide marketplace where small companies can compete head-to-head with large ones.

- Society has attacked the world of business. Just notice in the movies, songs, political speeches, etc., that it is always businessmen and the businesses themselves who are portrayed as 'evil' and the working man is always 'right.' *Think about it*: how often do you find yourself judging an 'evil' business entity in a movie? We are being programmed. If you do not think you are influenced, read Daniel Lapin's book, *Thou Shall Prosper*.[9]

- Legislation and government regulation meant to protect the people often result in businesses having to make adjustments which actually hurt those same people. Over the past 100 years, government has become increasingly involved in business. Much legislation makes it more expensive to hire and keep people on the payroll, so downsizing and outsourcing become a natural alternative for business survival.

- Lawsuits have companies running scared, so they have to build the cost of litigation into their pricing, and they have to be willing to hold their employees at arm's length to protect themselves from being sued for just doing business.

The result is a demand for high-quality goods and services with tough price competition in an environment of ever-increasing regulation and threats of legal actions. No longer can one company dominate and hold fast to large markets and employment sets. Many of the great companies of the past have either lost their edge or disappeared entirely. Why? Perhaps they tried to hold to a standard operating model too long—the economy is dynamic and they were static.

Great companies have struggled and new companies have emerged to take their markets away. Companies like Microsoft, Wal-Mart, Dell, and Cisco came in ready to embrace the changed economy and thrived. But today, even these new companies must struggle to keep up and keep ahead.

Companies must be dynamic. They no longer need "bodies" to work in factories for thirty years producing products. And they can no longer afford the cost of long-term retirements and pension plans, which have all but bankrupted the entire automotive industry. Instead, they need special talents to get things done.

Some projects last for years, others for months, but nothing in corporate America is 'permanent' anymore. People are no longer part of the family; they are simply a means to get work accomplished. Relationships still exist, but they are different now—not bad, just different. Just like two people in a relationship with differing expectations, the resulting stress can be very damaging.

NEW CORPORATE THINKING

In the past several years, several shake-ups have been experienced in the world of employment. We have watched as major companies have been purchased or merged with other companies, resulting in the loss of thousands of jobs.

Most of these major changes have been due to the desire to maximize profit. Others are driven by changes in market conditions and, at times, poor management. Some larger companies have simply lost their edge or suffered financially due to improper actions of their leaders.

But who *really* suffers? Clearly we can see suffering from the investors, the customers, and the employees. But there are global levels of suffering going on underneath. Think about the following impacts from our modern corporate culture:

- The changed view of individual employees. There is often a bitterness and complete distrust of "the company" being discussed in the offices of corporate America. Talk such as "this company doesn't care about us" and "I am sure the CEO (or other leader) is getting rich over this" is common in today's culture. Getting rich has become the evil instead of the dream!

- The disruption of life. Employees often know about, or at least suspect, a merger, acquisition, or reengineering project well before it is announced. Rumors of boardroom discussions as well as the ability to 'see the handwriting on the wall' result in employees being able to see a major change coming. As a result, many employees put major life decisions on hold as they wait to see what impact the changes will have on their everyday lives. They become people 'waiting to live' because their lives are being held captive by slow corporate decisions. The larger the company, the slower the actions and the greater number of people impacted.

- Corporate slavery. OK, not corporate slavery, but self-inflicted slavery to a company. The idea of "I have too much invested here to move on now" seems to prevail. I often hear comments like, "I have 15 years here and all I have to do is tough it out for another 15 to get retirement... they may make me an offer to retire early." Someone who barely missed a recent downsizing with the AT&T mergers told me, "I am just biding my time."

- Self identify crisis. Psychologists and self-improvement experts have convinced us that our work does not identify us. This is critical to the "self-esteem" of many since they have a need to distance themselves from what they do.

I understand that what you do does not provide your worth, yet the idea of trying to separate myself from my work is pretty crazy. It sounds like more politically correct thinking for those who are ashamed of their work.

My uncle, Charles Word, was a retired army general. Even years after retiring from the military, he would still answer the phone, "General Word." Why do you think he continued to identify with what he had been? Do you think Bill Gates wants us to think of him as just another man and not the founder of Microsoft? You see the point, I hope: people who are proud of what they do, or have done, are not afraid of their self-esteem being damaged by association with their work.

In all of history, people have been identified with what they do. Jesus was a carpenter. Napoleon was a military leader. Newton was a theologian and mathematician. Michelangelo was an artist. Historically, many cultures had family names based on their profession.

Jay Leno is a comedian; Miley Cyrus in a singer; Jim Carrey is an actor. We get that. They are proud of what they do to make a living. I remember running into a shoe man who said, "I repair people's soles." He was not ashamed; he was proud of his work. And what is it with so many women not wanting to say they are homemakers? What are they ashamed of, and why? This idea of a "self identify" crisis is true only when you are ashamed of your work. Why would anyone need to be ashamed if they are serving others?

- Lack of fulfillment. The average employee feels underpaid and under-appreciated. This is not to say that they want more money (though they do feel they deserve more for their efforts). They also *really* feel as though no one appreciates what they do—not the boss for sure, but often not even the customer. In fact, so many employees are so far removed from the customer they cannot see how their work is related to providing the customer with goods and services. The result is a lack of purpose for the corporate employee.

This corporate employee mindset seems to prevail in America today. No matter the company, no matter the industry, I find this kind of talk prevails in the employee base.

The term "TGIF" expresses a way to escape this ritual of daily self-defeat and self-inflicted suffering. Oh, wait, did I say self-inflicted? More on that later.

REALITY CHECK

While working at my telecom job, I was part of a control center that was under consideration for consolidation with other centers in the region. It was no secret that the company was considering the consolidation of all the centers for each state or for each region.

Yet, when the employees working in these centers inquired about the plans to consolidate the company, middle management suggested no such changes were on the table. (I knew this was a lie since I was on one of the committees drawing up the plans.)

These employees, many with 20+ years of service, were waiting for the official word to come down before they would make major financial decisions. Some, looking for a new home, delayed their search. Some, who were renting, decided not to buy. Some decided not to take expensive vacations. None of them knew how the inevitable changes would impact their future.

Basically, they put their lives on hold, for five years, while waiting for the decision to be made as to which centers stayed and which went.

TODAY'S PLAN FOR HAPPINESS

Why do so many people say, "I want out of corporate America" and "I want to be my own boss"? These two statements tend to bubble up out of the symptoms just described. How many of these symptoms have you personally felt or witnessed?

The model we have used has us working in a rat race, for sure. We educate for 16 years to prepare for work, get married, and have a family. We tend to work harder and harder, yet see less and less success coming our way. Then, we teach our kids to do the same. This circular race is why we call the American Dream the rat race. The problem is that most of us feel unfulfilled and without purpose in our corporate jobs. As Ken Blanchard says, "Even if you win the rat race, you are still a rat."

The term "TGIF" expresses a way to escape this ritual of daily self-defeat and self-inflicted suffering.

THE BRUTAL TRUTH

Jim Collins says in his book, *Good to Great*, that great leaders confront the brutal facts. In this case, the brutal facts reveal that most of us are playing by the wrong rulebook. How can we ever win if we do not even know the real rules? In the next few chapters, we will look at those real rules and become a Company of One!

DEVELOP YOUR COMPANY OF ONE

Consider how things have gone for you, and answer the following question in preparation for the next chapter.

Think of examples where other people were responsible for things that negatively impacted you. What was the result or impact to you? What is happening to you now that someone else is responsible for causing?

3

SIX ACTIONS THAT LEAD TO

SUCCESS

"Success is the progressive realization of a worthy goal."
Earl Nightingale[1]

So if success is not found from the magic formula we have been sold:

$$12 + 4 \neq success$$

Then how do we find success?

Mountains of research have been created on what makes people successful. In fact, we all have our own internal research factories. We know, or know of, happy and successful people.

Think about those you know. Can you determine the common denominator—the traits all successful people seem to have? Have you

noticed that success has little to do with circumstances such as **formal education, upbringing, family wealth, or many other factors?** You might also have noticed that success has little to do with the "job market" as defined by our educational system.

If you have not noticed these facts, then let me assure you that data collected from a wide range of people and over many years seem to point to the fact that the 12+4 strategy does *not* equal success. **In fact, 12+4 will likely result in you being an average, middle-class American who suffers from TGIF syndrome.** Instead, research on successful people has identified the following key actions.

ACTION 1

Successful people are not victims; they take responsibility for their lives

Steven Covey, author of *The 7 Habits of Highly Effective People*, notes that the word *responsibility* is a combination of the word RESPONSE and the word ABILITY. In other words, *you have the ability to respond to any event in a manner of your choosing*. Think about it. Remember the last time someone pulled out in front of you on the way to work when you were in a rush. The initial response in that type of situation is fear resulting in your hitting the brakes to avoid hitting the other driver. Then what happened? Did you fume about it all the way to work? Did you go to work still mad at what that idiot did? So often we do. We let other events control us. Think about this formula:

$$Event + Response = Outcome$$

Often, we have no control over the events in this equation. These events happen *to* us, usually not *because* of us. We may get laid off, get bumped from a flight, find ourselves in a traffic jam, etc. We may have no control over the event, yet the outcome is a result of the event *in conjunction with* the response (which we *do* control). We *can* control how we respond.

Too often we see external events destroy people and they go through life angry. But if they looked in the mirror they would see the other part of the problem: their own response.

THE BITTER PILL

I used to have an administrative assistant who worked for one other person besides me. I did not hire her—she had been around for years before me. She did an excellent job at everything she touched and really took excellent care of everyone. The problem was that she constantly complained about everything.

Everyone was 'out to get her.' Decisions were made about budgets that directly impacted her position and how she spent money. She was convinced that these things were done directly against her because "they just want to get rid of me."

I would tell her, "You may be right or you may be wrong, but what are you going to do? To complain about it will get you nowhere. Either quit and do what you want, or stay and be happy. Why be miserable?"

Of course, she would agree with me...and then go straight back to complaining. This was her MO—everything everyone did bothered her at a personal level.

She was so negative that I dreaded even seeing her. *Her* responses to external events were causing new events for *me!* I had to decide how to respond to her, and decided to always be upbeat and talk positively about everyone. She quickly decided that I was not sympathetic enough, so she wasted little time complaining to me. It is sad—such a remarkably talented and caring lady who was so bitter that no one wanted to work with her. She did not realize that she had the ability to respond differently.

WATCH YOUR LANGUAGE!

The point here is: we can respond to any event. Think about the people you know. Who are the 'bitter pills' in your life? How do you respond to them? Do you join in (negativity is contagious, you know), or do you choose to respond differently?

What about the people you know who can, and do, respond differently to events? Who do you know like that: people who, no matter what happens, look for (and often find) opportunity?

After coaching people for the past ten years, I have noticed that we often fall in love with what we hate. Time after time I meet with people who do not like their current situation and are ready to make a change. They devise a new plan to make a living doing something they love. Yet, over and over again during our meetings they spend most of the time rehashing complaints about their current job, boss, or work situation.

I find myself saying over and over again, "let's get back to the plan and stop focusing on what you are trying to get away from." If this is you, *watch your language*! Focus on solutions and plans, not complaining and blaming.

CANCELLED FLIGHTS REVEAL NEW OPPORTUNITY

In *Linchpin*, Seth Godin tells the story of Richard Branson being trapped in the Caribbean 40 years ago. Branson's flight (which was the only flight out for that day) had been canceled. Instead of reacting with anger, or pouting and complaining, Branson went to the charter desk, chartered a plane, then sold tickets to other stranded passengers. He ended up getting his flight for *free*! Years later, Branson started Virgin Airlines. Do you think that canceled flight sowed some seeds and taught him about the sale of airline tickets? Branson took action—he responded differently, and got a different, more positive, outcome.

WAR CARS

In his book, *The Success Principles*, Jack Canfield describes a friend of his who owns a Lexus dealership in Southern California. During the first Gulf War, economic uncertainty resulted in a reduced demand for luxury cars. All the dealers knew it and passively accepted this external event.

But his friend did *not* accept defeat so easily. He had his sales people take a fleet of cars to yacht clubs, golf courses, and country clubs. They let the members drive the cars around for a while just for fun. And you know what happened: when they got back in their own cars that did not smell as clean or seem as nice, they just *had* to buy a Lexus.

ACTION 2

Successful people have passion

Call it energy, drive, or ambition—successful people are focused on something they want. Think of sports figures. Michael Jordan and Tiger Woods (before his recent extracurricular activities) had a drive all their lives to excel at their chosen sport. They love it, work hard at it, and have a passion for their game. This is also true of Bill Gates and Steve Jobs. In fact, find a happy and fulfilled person and you will find passion.

THE DOOR MAN

A man named Bill Price goes to my church. Bill greets everyone at the door every Sunday, and has a passion and sense of purpose for this 'work' of greeting. Now there are a lot of people who "greet" people—think of WalMart greeters. But Bill is different. I stood at the door with him one morning and he told me about people who came through the door. He looked at their faces and tried to understand where they were. Were they happy or sad? Was something troubling them?

He told me his prayer was that God would give him the words to say to these people as they came in the door which would minister to their needs. Wow! I remember walking away from this seemingly meaningless post thinking this guy really gets it. He has a true passion and a true purpose, and he is making a positive impact on many lives every week.

He is not paid for this service, but is well known for it. In fact, he is so well respected and successful in his 'work' that the entrance of the church has become known as the "Bill Price Lobby." He is not just standing around; he is serving a mission and doing it with a passion.

THE JOBS PASSION

I recently watched the video of Steve Jobs' 2005 commencement address to Stanford. (There is a bit of irony about a man speaking at a college that would likely have rejected his application.) As I listened to him, I wondered how many of those graduates would go on to live a life with little meaning, believing in nothing, chasing only the almighty dollar, and working without passion. They wouldn't do this if they truly listened to Steve and took what he said to heart. He talked of following a passion as the key ingredient in life and in success.

Here is an excerpt from the speech where he described being fired from Apple. You can find the whole speech at the Stanford News Service website.

"...I didn't see it then, but it turned out that getting fired from Apple was the best thing that could have ever happened to me. The heaviness of being successful was replaced by the lightness of being a beginner again, less sure about everything. It freed me to enter one of the most creative periods of my life.

"During the next five years, I started a company named NeXT, another company named Pixar, and fell in love with an amazing woman who would become my wife. Pixar went on to create the world's first computer-animated feature film (Toy Story), and is now the most successful animation studio in the world. In a remarkable turn of events, Apple bought NeXT, I returned to Apple, and the technology we developed at NeXT is at the heart of Apple's current renaissance. And Laurene and I have a wonderful family together.

"I'm pretty sure none of this would have happened if I hadn't been fired from Apple. It was awful-tasting medicine, but I guess the patient needed it. Sometimes life hits you in the head with a brick. Don't lose faith. I'm convinced that the only thing that kept me going was that I loved what I did.

"You've got to find what you love. And that is as true for your work as it is for your lovers. Your work is going to fill a large part of your life, and the only way to be truly satisfied is to do what you believe is great work. And the only way to do great work is to love what you do. If you haven't found it yet, keep looking. Don't settle. As with all matters of the heart, you'll know when you find it. And, like any great relationship, it just gets better and better as the years roll on. So keep looking until you find it. Don't settle."

ACTION 3

Successful people have vision

Successful people know what they are after and they see something others do not. Jim Carrey was one of these people. While a 'starving artist', Carrey envisioned himself as a highly paid and highly sought-after actor. He was known to carry a check in his wallet written to himself for $10,000,000—the memo said "for acting services."

Every day he looked at that check and imagined receiving it for his role in movies. Some may have thought he was crazy, but his vision carried him forward. His 2009 movie, *Yes Man,* earned him over $28 million. The check in his wallet did not get him there—his drive and the focus of his vision helped him succeed in a business where most fail. Talk to any highly successful person and you'll learn of their vision.

WEIGHTLIFTER TO POLITICIAN

We all know Arnold Schwarzenegger as the internationally-known-bodybuilder-turned-movie-star-turned-politician. At first glance it might appear that Arnold just wandered from one success to another. Yet, his raw determination and strong vision created his successes.

As a teenager, Arnold's soccer coach sent him to the weight room to improve his conditioning. He became hooked. At the gym, he found a poster of Reg Park, a bodybuilder playing the part of Hercules in a movie. Reg had won the Mr. Universe title in bodybuilding and then turned it into a movie career.

Arnold then knew what his dream was: to win Mr. Universe, then become a movie star and get rich. At age twenty, Arnold told a friend, "I want to win Mr. Universe many times like Reg. I want to go into film like Reg; I want to be a billionaire; I want to go into politics."[3]

We all can look at Arnold's career to date and see how he moved from one successful role to another, but we do not see the many struggles he encountered along the way. How many setbacks did he have to overcome? Like you and me, he had many. He even "took off a few days" during his service in the Austrian Army (without permission) to enter and win a bodybuilding contest in Germany—an act that landed him in jail for a week. Arnold felt it was a sacrifice he had to take to reach his goal. Arnold's burning vision kept him focused on his goals. (By the way, he is not a billionaire yet—he is *only* worth $800 million, so he still has work to do.)

ACTION 4

Successful People Take Risks

Do you ever make mistakes? Do you ever cast a vision for something to happen, tell it to the world, and then fall on your face? Do you ever step up, then fail? For some of you, the answer is 'rarely.' And because you rarely fail, you feel successful, maybe even superior.

Yet, we find people of great success often have had a string of failures before they found their way to the top. We love to highlight failure and laugh in the face of others' failings, but what we love even more is success. When people overcome failure and setbacks, they tend to forget about the difficulties along the way.

Think about how many times a famous musical group appears to rise to stardom as an overnight success. When you hear them interviewed, you learn that their rise was anything but overnight—they played for years and years in small clubs before they 'hit the big time.'

Dan Miller had a recent blog post in which he highlighted the following successful people and their views on failure:[4]

"Would you like me to give you a formula for success? It's quite simple, really. Double your rate of failure. You are thinking of failure as the enemy of success. But it isn't at all. You can be discouraged by failure, or you can learn from it. So go ahead and make mistakes. Make all you can. Because, remember that's where you will find success." –Thomas J. Watson, Sr., founder and former CEO of IBM

"He who never made a mistake never made a discovery." –Samuel Smiles, Scottish author and reformer

"While one person hesitates because he feels inferior, the other is busy making mistakes and becoming superior." –Henry C. Link, leading psychologist in the 1930s and author of Return to Religion

"I've missed more than 9,000 shots in my career. I've lost almost 300 games. 26 times, I've been trusted to take the game-winning shot and missed. I've failed over and over and over again in my life. And that is why I succeed." Michael Jordan (no introduction needed)

So cast a big vision and decide *not* to live on the safe side, but decide what you want to do, go after it, and do not be afraid of failure—in fact, embrace it.

ACTION 5

Successful people set goals

Successful people actively set goals for themselves. This is a simple, yet powerful, statement. We all know people who make lists and write out their goals. In fact, we often make fun of them. But the fact is that a reasonable amount of evidence suggests that setting goals is a major key to success.

Do *you* set goals? If not, clearly you need to learn how. If you do, how safe are your goals? At first glance many goals seem bizarre and way out of the reach of the people who make them. But think about it—even if they fall short of their goal, what will they have achieved?

THE RIGHT KIND OF FAILURE

Jack Canfield, co-author of the series, *Chicken Soup for the Soul*, relates how he set a goal to make $100,000 in one year. He was making $25,000 per year at the time, and to him (and many around him) the $100,000 goal was a leap. And, yes, that first year he did fall short of his goal—he made only $92,000.[5] Sure, he failed...but we should all fail so successfully!

Even though he missed that goal, it propelled him forward. In fact, his wife was so inspired by the "success" of his goal that she suggested the next goal should be one million per year—which he did achieve, and has ever since.

MAKE YOUR OWN RULES

One of the problems I have always had is that what I want to achieve often gets in the way of how I want to live. I prefer to be with my family. But many people tell me that the only way to succeed is to travel—to be *away* from family.

One of the most eye-opening moments I've ever had hit me when I had lunch with Dan Miller. I had heard Dan on the radio with Dave Ramsey, then I bought his book and read it. I loved it.

Dan was doing something similar to what I wanted to do, so I just had to talk to him. I sent an email to the only address on his website and told him that I wanted to buy him lunch. The email went something like, *"I will be in the Nashville area soon and would like to buy his lunch and pick his brain on some topics."*

I got a very nice email back from his handlers (as I expected) thanking me on Dan's behalf for contacting him. I searched for a phone number, only to get stopped by a voicemail system. So I persisted with another email:

> *I would like to meet Dan. I am in B'ham and I would be happy to come to Nashville to meet over coffee or lunch. I am looking to do something very similar to what he's doing and love his work. I would just like to pick his brain a bit about what and how he has done it. After all, requesting a meeting is exactly what he would advise.*

That worked! In a few days I got an email back from Dan to line up a lunch. I went to meet him and he shared with me that his company consisted of only two people—and one of them was *him*! The first email had been sent by his daughter, the handler. "So," I said, "the whole big company image is for show?" He laughed and explained that he and Dave Ramsey had gone broke about the same time, and wanted to start businesses doing something very similar. Dave wanted to have a large company with a large staff. Dan said he wanted something very different: he had large staffs before and wanted a small team this time. He explained that he has dozens—maybe even hundreds—of people working for him on contract, but only one person on salary. He wanted it that way!

It was an eye-opener to learn that he did not listen to others about *how* to do his business—he did it on his own terms. Both he and Dave Ramsey succeeded—*on their own terms*—in similar businesses, yet they operate their businesses very differently. Dave works out of an office with a staff; Dan works out of his home with almost no staff.

Though he did not mean to be offering advice (he was just telling his story), this single event has had a dramatic impact on me. Whenever I hear people say, "the only way to succeed in X is to do Y," I just think about Dan and Dave, and say to myself, "I bet you are wrong."

ACTION 6

Successful people EXECUTE

The ultimate reality check: success takes work. I have read many books on success over the years. I really enjoy the insights and find them inspiring. However, I rarely achieve more success just from reading! It is like trying to lose weight by reading exercise and diet books—it doesn't work. As my wife has been famous for telling our children, "it is fine to *dream* big, but to make it happen you have to *work* big!"

ABD

I was ABD (a term well known to PhD students which stands for "All But Dissertation"—or All But Done). A doctoral program often involves several courses and then a dissertation, which is the final lap for the PhD student. The faculty controls the coursework—they set the agenda, teach the material, give the assignments and tests, and at the end of the term they give the grade. If you are a PhD student, you follow directions and do the work.

The dissertation is different. Some candidates are fortunate in that their advisor sets a plan and demands what they want. Many candidates complain about how unreasonable their advisors are as they demand more and more. In reality, though, the PhD student who does *not* have this kind of advisor will almost never finish.

The coursework is easy, but at this point in the program, the candidate has to set their own direction, and no one cares whether they finish or not. I am guessing there are a hundred ABD PhD candidates for every PhD graduate—and I was about to join that majority.

It was a Saturday in August 1999. I had been ABD for a few years. We had just moved to a new house and I was setting up an office for my consulting work. I came across all my PhD notes and work in progress. I looked at Lea (my wife) and told her I was going to dump this out and forget it. I had long ago lost interest.

She looked at me, and in her submissive, gentle words, said, "You are an idiot!" OK, I'm not sure exactly what she said, but that is what I *heard*. She went on to say, "you've done all the other work and all you have to do now is complete one simple document and you're done."

I had never quite heard a dissertation described as a 'simple document'! I started to argue, but then realized she *might* be right. She then followed with the words that made all the difference: "*You have to just make it happen!*"

I decided right then that I would take the first two hours of each day to do just that: *make it happen*. If I had to get up early or bill fewer consulting hours, I would make it happen. Some days took more than two hours, some less, but as time went on, the momentum shifted and I became a machine focused on finishing.

Nothing was in the way anymore. I became a pain-in-the-rear to my advisors—making them read my stuff and provide me with feedback. Within one month, I was nearly done with all but the politics. From then on, minor edits, meetings, and a presentation were all that remained to be done.

I finished so quickly that I actually had to stop and wait because the rule was that candidate could not graduate until nine months after deciding on their topic. I had chosen my topic in August and was ready to go by November.

EXECUTION

The word is EXECUTION. Ask all successful entrepreneurs what made the difference. Why did one company make it and the other never got off first base? The reasons for failure are always listed in the top ten things they did wrong, but the fact is that *they failed to execute*. They did not decide, and then follow through, in order to make it happen.

Dreams are important. Attitude is critical. Without these, you will end up passively accepting and compromising. Success requires action! And, we all know, the hardest action of all is setting the destination and finding the drive to accomplish it all. This is why we hire life and career coaches and personal trainers—we need someone to set the agenda for us and kick us in the rear to make it happen.

WHY?

So why have I spent time talking about success? First, to demonstrate that success is not a degree or a pedigree—common sense stuff is what breeds success. We all have *that*! Second, we need to see that success is within reach of us all. We are in control. Third, we determine our own goal! *We* get to define what makes us successful. We do *not* have to live by the world's definition of success; instead, we create our own vision and goals.

> *Success is not a degree or a pedigree- common sense stuff is what breeds success. We all have that!*

You can have success, too! You don't have to feel trapped. No tuition is needed, and no long hours studying facts are required. **Just start now.**

DEVELOP YOUR COMPANY OF ONE

1. Quickly write down what three goals you want to accomplish in the next year or two. You know what they are—write them down. Now, do you remember your weekly To Do list from Chapter 1? How many things on that list map to the goals you just wrote down? Your yearly goals are what you're aiming for, but your weekly list shows how you will spend your time getting there.

2. Revisit your Chapter 1 list of events where other people were responsible for results in your life. Using something that's happening to you now as an example, write down, "*I am responsible!*" Then consider, as the responsible party should, how you choose to view this situation now. Is there action you should take? Is an opportunity presenting itself? How have other people been impacted, including the person you hold responsible?

3. What is your passion? If money were not an object, what would you do with your time?

4. Who are the people in your life whom you consider successful? Meet with two of these people to discover their vision and goals.

4

YOUR COMPANY OF ONE

"Every day I get up and look through the Forbes list of the richest people in America. If I'm not there, I go to work." Robert Orben[1]

What is the *true* American dream? When I ask, many people tell me it's working for themselves. When I ask why they want to work for themselves, their reasons vary, until it comes to finances. At that point, the main reasons I hear are:

"I want the ability to earn more money."

"I want to earn my own way and not have my income artificially controlled by external events."

"Control of the outcome is what I am after. I know I can do a better job than my employer does at creating income and taking care of customers."

Sometimes I get answers which I believe are the *true* reasons:

> *"I want control of my time and my life. I hate being tied to a clock to meet the world's timetable even when my job does not really require it."*

> *"Freedom is my number-one goal. When it comes time to go to an event for my son, I want to be able to do it."*

Talk to people who have developed substantial wealth and you'll discover that they place great value on their time and their freedom. So perhaps the true American Dream is Freedom! Alan Weiss in his book, *Million Dollar Consulting*, says it well:

> *"Real wealth is discretionary time, being able to do what you desire when you desire to do it, whether it's watching our kids' soccer games and dance recitals or creating a new client proposal. You can always earn more money, but you can't make more time."* [2]

THE MONEY FLOW MODEL

To understand the meaning of self-employment, look at a simple diagram of corporate money flow:

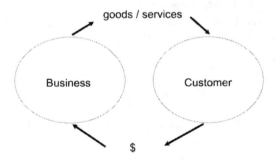

Notice the key is the goods or services that are exchanged for money. Simple. This model is how our economy operates. The diagram is the same no matter if the company is on the *Fortune* 100 list or is a self-employed yardman.

But now let's look at what most of us in corporate America are doing. It's a diagram of the employee/employer relationship:

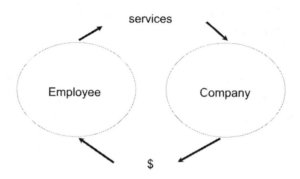

Notice that, once again, goods and services (usually services) are being exchanged for money. But look closely! The diagram is the same. See it? The financial transaction is the same. The company in the second model becomes the customer of the first model. The employee of the second model becomes the business of the first model. The fact is, besides some tax treatment and bookkeeping issues, the two models are identical!

CONGRATULATIONS, YOU ARE SELF-EMPLOYED

If you are taking in money right now for the work you perform, you are self-employed.

Yes, if you are taking in money right now for the work you perform, you are self-employed. That is just how our economy works. So let us consider some ideas here. First, let the company in the first diagram be WalMart. We are all familiar with WalMart, and most of us spend more time in the store than we like to admit. But, at any time and for any reason, WalMart could refuse to serve you.

For instance, assume their new CEO hates LSU. The CEO could implement a policy refusing to allow entrance to the store to anyone wearing an LSU jersey—or even the LSU colors. Think about it now—they could legally do that! They might get sued and receive some bad PR, but they certainly could do that and have every right to do it—they own the business.

Likewise, you could, for any reason, refuse to shop in WalMart ever again. Your reason does not have to be logical—it is still *your* reason. Therefore, either you or the business could decide to sever the relationship at any time and for any reason.

Now look at the second (employer) model. Do you have the right to quit your job for any reason? What if your boss is a hockey fan? You hate hockey and may refuse to work for anyone who watches or participates in the sport, so you decide to quit. You have every right to do that.

> The only difference between you and an entrepreneur is that you have chosen to sell all of your services (your time) to a single customer.

Also (and you might not like this one as much), they have every right to fire *you* for any reason. If you show up to work in a red shirt, they could fire you because the boss decided that morning that he hates red. In most every state in the US, he has the right to do that—it's called "at-will" employment. You and the employer can sever the relationship at your own will and for your own reasons. (I understand some employers also have non-discrimination issues they must adhere to, but not all of them!).

I know some of you might find this hard to believe, because we hear about wrongful termination lawsuits all the time. True, either of you could sue the other. You could sue for wrongful termination and they could sue you (if you quit) for some type of contract abandonment. If you get lawyers involved, anything can happen. And because of lawyers, employers are very careful how and why they hire and fire. The fact is that *your employer is your customer.* And just as in any customer/business relationship, both parties can decide to quit at any time for any reason.

YOUR CUSTOMERS

Let this sink in for a minute. Think about the implications. Your employer (even the employer you may hate) is your customer. Remember the times you complain about them. Think about the questions from Chapter 1 where you examined the frustrations you have with your employer. For many of you, you hate to see or hear from your boss. Can you imagine the CEO of WalMart thinking, "I hate people showing up in our stores; I just wish they would stay home!" Of course not. When customers show up, money changes hands. When you have customers and you do your work, money changes hands.

But there is another question here: can you write down who your customer is on a sheet of paper? Not the company name, but the *people.* Who has the power to fire you? Who has a major influence in how you are viewed? Who is your customer? This question is often a difficult one to answer in large organizations, but it's a very important one.

YOUR TIME

There is one notable difference between the company and employee models I have not yet pointed out, and it is a key one: *if you are employed, you have* one *customer who is the source of* all *your income.* But businesses such as WalMart, or smaller companies owned by entrepreneurs, have many customers.

The implications of these customers are pretty powerful. Let's say your neighbor mows yards for a living. Your neighbor could lose a customer for any reason—he may get fired for doing a poor job, his customer may move, or his customer might decide to buy their own lawnmower and start mowing their own yard for exercise. When he loses one customer, he has many others that still provide him with income.

If you work for a mega company, you, too, could lose your "customer" for many reasons—you may get fired for lack of performance; you may get downsized; you may lose your job when the company leaves town.

But the problem is that when you lose your customer, you have lost *all* your income! The only difference between you and an entrepreneur is that you have chosen to sell all of your time to a single customer.

Notice what I said, *you have chosen*! Let this sink in. Now we need to address how you are managing *your* company.

HOW DO YOU SHOW YOUR VALUE TO THE ORGANIZATION?

What value do you add to your employer? How do you either bring in income or generate savings for the company? Are these numbers higher than the salary they pay you? I ask these questions often and get a variety of reactions. Some claim they do not need to know this because they are employees, not contractors or consultants. Others tell me they cannot measure their role since they have no direct impact on the bottom line.

Yet, I find many CEOs who can tell me (to the penny) the economic impact of every employee in their company. Judy is the CEO of a mid-sized company. (I have changed her name to protect the innocent—or the guilty.) Judy has shown me a spreadsheet looking something like this:

Name	Salary	Benefits	Total Cost	Value to the Company	Difference
Henry Staff	$60,000	$15,000	$75,000	$350,000	$275,000
Jessica Smith	$85,000	$21,250	$106,250	$150,000	$43,750
Joe Ford	$75,000	$18,750	$93,750	$975,000	$881,250
Jeff Stevens	$100,000	$25,000	$125,000	$120,000	-$5,000

You can see from this table that Judy is tracking the total cost of each employee on her payroll. You see their salary and the cost of their benefits (including vacation, healthcare, 401k, etc.) which are typically

about 25% of salary. We often don't think of benefits being part of our income, but your employer thinks about it, because benefits cost them real dollars.

Next we see the CEO's valuation of what each employee brings to the company. This may be how much they sold or how much they saved, but note that it is measured in dollars. It then takes simple subtraction to see who is adding to the company's bottom line.

From the above example, we see that Joe Ford is a superstar. If he knows about her measure of his performance, he is going to be asking for a *big* raise. Then consider her highest paid employee, Jeff. He is costing the company—he's money lost. If I were Judy, I would be thinking about letting Jeff go. Nothing personal, just business—that is, unless your name is Jeff Stevens.

The key is that she is measuring each employee's impact on the bottom line, and so is *your* employer! Your boss may not have a measure that looks just like this, but they had better have *some* measure!

Are Judy's numbers correct? Who knows? Let's face it, we (as customers ourselves) often fire vendors and service providers when we feel they fail to add value to our lives. You may fire your cable TV company based on the "feeling" that you just do not value their services anymore. You are not obligated to show them a spreadsheet—you just feel it. Why do you think *your* customer would be any different?

So, to simplify, your value-added equation needs to look like this (where V is the Value you bring to the company in the form of income or money saved, and C is your total cost to the company including salary and benefits):

$$V > C$$

REACTION

When I cover this material in classes and seminars, I get a variety of responses, but often I see an expression of deep thought and concern on the faces of the participants. The information is so obvious. They know this is correct, but they have either never thought of it this way or they have forgotten that they once did!

What about you? Are you concerned? Are you a little nervous? All is OK—the key is that simply by *knowing*, you are ahead of the game. Now you can control the game!

WHAT NOW?

So what do you do? Do the same things companies do! Develop a solid strategy to identify your customers, determine what they value about you, learn how they measure value, and continually demonstrate your value to them.

First, know your customers. No, I do not mean your employer's customers, but the one who is measuring *you*. It doesn't matter if you are an entrepreneur, a contractor, a consultant, or an employee—the same basic principles apply.

> So what do you do? Do the same things companies do! Develop a solid strategy to identify your customers, determine what they value about you, learn how they measure value, and continually demonstrate your value to them.

Someone is your customer: the one who gives you cash in return for goods and services. You may call them 'customer', 'boss', 'manager', 'company', or another term. In some cases, like that of an entrepreneur or consultant, you might have multiple customers that you must treat as a group. A key step to keeping the money rolling your way is to get inside the head of your customers, but you cannot do that until you know who they are.

In larger organizations, this can be a challenge since you might play a variety of roles and have multiple lines of management. You may also have peers who are key customers. But, the clearer you understand your role, the easier you can show your added value. You must know who is evaluating you and what value you add to the company.

Second, find out what matters to your customer(s). How? *Go ask them*. To get under the surface of the many statistical measurements that may or may not really matter, ask them some key questions:

- What are the key things you expect from me?
- What struggles are you having related to your job or your customers?
- What keeps you awake at night?
- How do you measure my value? (Try to see if they measure in dollars.)

Be aware: some customers may be taken aback by these questions (especially if your customer happens to be a middle manager). They themselves may not know what matters and what is value added—if so, this is a real problem for you. They may not even know what matters to their own boss (customer) and therefore your whole department could be in jeopardy. So if you do not get good answers, keep looking for new ways to ask. You may have to talk to the next level of bosses (customers) to see if you can understand how you and your group add value to the company.

REALITY CHECK

In a past work life, I spent much of my time tracking data on various measures of telecommunications equipment performance thinking I was doing what mattered. In fact, I knew I was; it was my job. Yet, the boss never seemed happy with the numbers. When I finally asked what really mattered, I found out he was being hammered from above by customer outage issues.

All of our measures were important, but the numbers did not have a predictable relationship to customer service. I find this type of situation in many companies I consult with, both large and small. Knowing what matters to your customer is key to making sure the work you are doing is something of value.

A word of caution is due here: many people tell me they already know what their customer wants, so they claim they do not need to ask. Perhaps they are correct, but this is a dangerous assumption. Marketing groups of well-known companies such a WalMart and Coca-Cola spend millions trying to learn what creates value for customers. They know that what customers value can change over time, so these groups continually ask questions to make sure they are in line with customer demands.

Why do you think you are any different? You are a company. Who is doing your market research?

Third, align your efforts with your customers' needs. Now that you know what matters to your customers, determine how well you are meeting their needs. What are you doing every day and how does it add value to what your customer cares about? When I discovered that my boss cared more about customer service than managing numbers, I made sure our telecom customers knew we cared and I intended to fix their problems quickly.

Life with my boss improved, and as it turns out, I was then adding real value—a big change from just pushing numbers as I had been doing before. (No, in case you're wondering, this was *not* one of the managers who voted me off the island.)

Fourth, find your number. Yes, back to that question: "How much value do you bring to the company?" Can you put some numbers on how much money you earn or save the company? I know, for some of you this can be challenging, but trust me, you need a number. After all, what if your customer does not have a number to measure your value? What if you are working in a support role? If your customer does not have a number, you can share yours with them. (Of course, only do this if the value you bring is more than the money they spend on your services!)

The funny thing is that data talks—even if it is not perfect. Your customer may challenge your assumptions, and you may learn how to improve how to calculate your number, but the key is that you now have a number. If your number does turn out to be lower than what you cost, start looking for ways to add more value or start looking for another customer!

ANTI-LINCHPIN?

Now, before I go on with this, I need to state that some people might disagree. In his book, *Linchpin*, Seth Godin points out that the value of a linchpin (the invaluable people in every company who cannot be replaced) may not be easy to measure. They may be people who are so good at working with customers that customers keep coming back and complaints go down, making them difficult to replace. But I think what Seth means is that it can be difficult to measure their value. I can measure customer retention and the value of reduced complaints, and so can you. It may not be easy and the measure may not be 100% accurate, but it *can* be measured in dollars!

HOW TO GET YOUR NUMBER

Let me walk through an example. To make it more complex, let's use a linchpin example:

Joe works as a support person for Softbake, LLC, a company that sells management software subscriptions to bakeries. Let's assume the software costs $120 per month per bakery. Joe is one of five people who handles calls from customers. All of Joe's customers and all of Joe's coworkers know he is "the man." He has a way of dealing with customers so even the angry ones are beaming with joy after talking with him.

But who cares what those customers who call support think? If Joe gets fired because his employer feels he's not adding value, those customers calling support do not matter. Joe needs to know how he is measured (in dollars) by *his* customer!

Joe can create a value model by taking the total number of customers using Softbake software and the total number of customers who call for support on a monthly basis. He can then estimate the number of customers who are happy with the support they got, the number who will buy again from them, and the number who would recommend them to others. He can look at the customers who were lost and the last support calls they made. Did *he* ever lose customers? Did the other support personnel lose any? What is the cost of losing a customer?

So here is what he might end up with:

calls Joe took last month: 250

Average customers lost after a typical support call: 15%
(if Joe were average, he should have lost 37.5 customers)

Actual customers Joe lost: 2

% of customers Joe lost: 2/250 = 0.8%

cost of losing a customer (one year of revenue): $1,440

Joe's value = $1,440 x (37.5 - 2) = $51,120

Now Joe also may have made some sales and had other things he could add to the equation. He might want to consider the total number of calls handled per month, etc. Are his numbers accurate? Who knows? But if he is the only one with numbers, people listen.

Note that when Joe starts this process, his co-workers will notice and he could find himself measuring value for the entire support team. Then he will likely want to find out how he can add *even more* value. He might suggest surveying customers, training the team on what he does that works, and looking at ways to up-sell customers during support calls.

Just by taking a look at what matters to the company (his real customer) he can begin to look at his job in new ways and add value. He could move from being a normal linchpin to a titanium linchpin!

Fifth, do little things that keep selling your value. You know buyer's remorse: you buy a new car and soon after start thinking that you really should have spent less money. Then the dealer calls to remind you of how highly rated and safe your car is (reminding you of its value) and you feel better.

Do this for your customers—remind them often of the value you bring to them. How you do this can vary, *but do it!* Buying your services is an expensive proposition, and you had better believe that someone in your line of customers asks the question often, "do we really need that person or that division?" Buyer's remorse is a human emotion related to spending money—and not just on cars.

Also, think about ways you can easily add extra value. Do you have data which can be used to provide valuable information? Can you generate a report that your boss can provide to his or her boss? In your interactions with customers, can you provide sales opportunities? Think about Amazon's "New for You" service—they know what you have bought in the past, and point out similar items that might interest you. They already have this data about you and are providing the extra service with little effort on their part. And, of course, the value they add to you often returns value to them!

> Remember— it is critical to know who your customer is and what matters to them.

Remember, we are all in the business of marketing our services to our customers. It is critical to know who your customer is and what matters to them. When we have delivered the goods, we then need to remind them of the value we have added. *Tell* your customer(s) how you are and adding value.

BUT...

I know what many of you are thinking: my current position is *not* my dream job! That's OK for now. These concepts continue to play out and understanding the process is critical, so when you *do* land your dream job, you will know how to make it count. Right now the key is to know *you are a Company of One!*

Go through the exercise covered in this chapter and the next. Take the time to really think it through. Remember, *the thinking is more important than the reading*. In the next few chapters, we will begin to move you from an average Company of One to a stellar Company of One. And more important, we will begin to define and move toward that work which you are truly called to do and will love doing.

DEVELOP YOUR COMPANY OF ONE

Answer the following questions, keeping in mind that you are self-employed:

- What business are you in?
- Who are your customers?
- What are you selling?
- Are you doing to your customer what you complained about your boss/employer doing to you? (Remember those questions you answered at the very beginning?)

Now go ask your customers the following:

- What are the key things you expect from me?
- What struggles are you having related to your job or your customers?
- What keeps you awake at night?
- How do you measure value?
- What is the value of the services I provide to you? (Try to get to dollars if possible.)

5

MANAGING YOUR

COMPANY OF ONE

"Nothing so conclusively proves a man's ability to lead others as what he does from day to day to lead himself." ~Thomas J. Watson[1]

Now that you see you are a company and you have some ideas, let's look at your board of directors.

FUNCTIONS OF YOUR COMPANY

Every company has four key functions:

Operations—Operations are the everyday events of keeping the company going and serving customers. For WalMart, operations involves making sure the doors are open in the morning, making sure employees are in the store, maintaining inventory on the shelves, keeping the power and phones working, etc. Operations is a big job in most companies. We will call the person responsible for this job the **COO, or Chief Operations Officer.** In your company, *you* are the COO.

Finance—The finance function takes in the money and pays the bills. They look at how to measure profits, and keep a watch on what is profitable and what is not. They also report financial data to legal entities (IRS) and stakeholders (owners). We will call this person the **CFO, or Chief Financial Officer**. In your company, *you* are the CFO.

Research and Development—We all know of research and development as R&D. Though we most often think of these people as developing new technology and patents, I am using R&D in a larger sense. R&D is always on the lookout for new things to offer to customers—things that can improve service and things that can reduce costs. At the same time they must be watching the business environment to learn what the competition is doing and what threats are on the horizon. So R&D may have plans for less than one-year implementations of new processes as well as five-year plans. We will call the person in charge of R&D the **CRO, or Chief Research Officer**. In your company, *you* are the CRO.

Marketing and Sales—This is the group of people who are key to bringing home the money. They are responsible for presenting the product to the market, knowing what the market wants, offering input about future products, dealing with customer satisfaction, dealing with "buyer's remorse," and generally protecting the image of the company. We will call this person the **CMO, or Chief Marketing Officer**. In your company, *you* are the CMO.

The Buck Stops Here—Every company has a leader, and the leader is responsible for working with the people who represent and implement the four key functions. The leader is ultimately responsible for it all. They work with the team to form a strategy. We will call this person the **CEO, or Chief Executive Officer**. In your company—you guessed it—*you* are the CEO.

THE BOARD

Collectively these people—the CEO, COO, CFO, CMO, and CRO—form what is called the Board of Directors (or simply the Board). They, as a group, make the company succeed or fail. Many companies may also have outsiders on their board—people who have a vested interest (such as investors, other owners, or stockholders) or people who can give trusted advice (such as leaders from other companies who have been tested and can provide valuable input).

DEVELOP YOUR COMPANY OF ONE

So what about *your* Board? How do the functions of a major company, such as Coca-Cola, translate to the functions of your Company of One? We will go into more detail later but, for now, answer the following questions:

1. Who is on your Board? Who else (besides you) is a trusted advisor, investor, stockholder, or stakeholder of your Company of One? (Your spouse and family are considered stakeholders.)

2. For your Company of One, write out each role and some things you feel you are doing in each. Note areas where you feel strong and others where you feel weak.

6

COO FOR YOUR COMPANY OF

ONE

"Success isn't a result of spontaneous combustion. You must set yourself on fire." Arnold H. Glasow [1]

Let's begin to dissect how you are operating your company and learn how to really make things work for you. Note again that if you are not happy with your current job, take heart. Right now we are dealing with what brings in your money today; we will begin to *really* plan what you want to do in the future very soon. But learning how to operate your company now will make your desired career path easier to reach later.

> Learning how to operate your company now will make your desired career path easier to reach later.

WHAT THE COO DOES

Do you know what is involved in company operations? Do we know what kind of tasks a chief operating officer performs for his or her employer? The COO role is perhaps the most critical function in the day-to-day operation of the company. Everything that happens is caused, or at least impacted by, the operations person.

Think in terms of a retail store. The COO role makes sure the store is open and open on time. They also make sure employees are present, inventory is in the store, and the systems are operating. Perhaps most critical of all, the COO is often the person in charge of the interaction between the customer and the business!

The left side of the chart on the following pages shows a few of the responsibilities of a typical company COO. This list is far from complete, and certainly not all companies are run the same way, but, generally, the COO is responsible for the day-to-day operations of the company.

The right-hand column shows you the equivalent operations for your Company of One. Again, this will vary, but the idea is that in your Company of One you have areas of responsibility, and only *you* are responsible.

Now let's look at your role as COO of your Company of One.

First, you have to be able to get to the location where you perform your services. That means you have to have your business ready to run when business starts. For many of us, business begins in the morning. You need the ability to get to work, so that means the COO is responsible for maintaining their body and their car!

If you do not show up to work on time because your car failed to perform, you are responsible and your customer may suffer. If you oversleep because you were out late at a party the night before, again your customer could suffer.

Typical Company	Company of One
Open and close the business daily	Show up to work
Keep inventory in stock	Communicate with your customers about the services you perform
Keep supplies needed to operate	Do your "job"
Make delivery of products and supplies	Take care of your ability to get to work (your car?)
Interface to customers during the "goods/services" transaction	Take care of the inventory (in a service business, that's *you*)
Present the proper image by keeping the store/office neat and clean	Present the professional image you want to communicate to your customers
Handle customer complaints	Deal with your customers on complaints and lack of satisfaction with your work
Make the customer feel welcome	Make your customers feel good about having you around by being pleasant and encouraging

Think about this: if you had a meeting scheduled with an accountant at your house, what would you think if they showed up late with bloodshot eyes from staying up too late the night before? Or suppose they show up late with a car smoking and dripping oil in your driveway. Will you make a judgment about their professional ability? You know you would, and you would be right—they have failed to run their company professionally.

THE LOOK

What about your dress? If you go to a grocery store you expect employees to be dressed nicely, maybe even in uniform. If the cashiers look ragged, what will you think? How have you decided to dress at work? Have you dropped your standards over time, relaxing to the lowest common denominator? How does your boss dress? How about those at the highest management levels? What image do you really want for your Company of One?

I am not suggesting that you must dress in formal business attire, but I *am* suggesting you need to dress in a manner that reflects your desired image for your Company of One. Just like going into the grocery store, everything the employees say and do brands the store. Likewise, everything *you* say, everything *you* do, and everything *you* wear brands *your* Company of One.

REALITY CHECK

A few years after I graduated from college and was working at BellSouth, I started noticing how people behaved when I dressed differently. I would dress in a normal relaxed shirt and tie to attend a meeting, and I took careful note of how I was treated. Then I would show up the next day (with the same people) wearing a dark suit with a red tie. At first I got lots of comments and questions such as, "who are you interviewing with today?"

As the day wore on, that question disappeared, and I noticed that I was being treated differently. I seemed to have more authority, and my words were doubted less often. When I gave a direction, I got immediate action instead of being challenged (which had been typical). Even the bosses seemed to act differently around me. If I went to the grocery store, I was treated with respect there, too. Your dress impacts you as well as others, so you need to think about the image you want to convey, and decide how you want to be treated.

Now I know what you're thinking: Steve Jobs shows up at his office in jeans, and if jeans are good enough for Steve, then they are good enough for you. I agree. But that is part of his brand and perhaps part of the Apple brand—it is a relaxed and fun company and we like that when we buy a technology tool. But would you want that image representing you in court? An attorney who shows up in jeans might be kicked out of court. But, even if the judge didn't mind, the jury might not see that attorney as credible. If the President showed up at the State of the Union address dressed like Steve Jobs, it would not go over well. You get my point.

So, you have to decide on the brand for your Company of One. What do you want your wardrobe to communicate about you? Decide now, because it communicates volumes.

CUSTOMER RELATIONS

One critical role of the COO is to take quality care of the customer. The COO is responsible for getting the work done and, like it or not, they are usually getting it done in front of the customer. In most companies, the COO is in control of the front line and represents the company's image to the world while getting the job done.

Southwest Airlines has become famous—and made lots of money—by treating customers well. Some airlines treat you as though getting on a plane were like going to a spa—as if they expected you to *enjoy* being herded like cattle. In a stressful time of airports, travel, and late flights, Southwest does not attempt to sugarcoat the fact that you would rather be doing something other than being packed into a thin tube and tossed into the air. They make traveling with them fun. Their light-hearted and fun approach makes the whole experience of travel a little more tolerable. And they perform with excellence—this is a must.

How do *your* customers feel about doing business with you? Do you make them feel welcome and do they know you are willing to help them? Or do you make them feel like they are interrupting you and are an annoyance? WalMart has greeters, and the idea is that they make customers feel welcome. How do you greet your customers?

SOMEONE IS WATCHING YOU

You are always being watched. Think about someone being on the news after being caught on video doing something illegal, unethical, or just plain embarrassing by a fellow citizen with a video camera. How would you feel if you were being recorded and what you said and did was shown to the world?

Well, like it or not, the same type of judgments are being made about you all the time. People are watching you now and they always have been. We all form opinions of others, it's normal. We tend to form immediate judgments. A book *is* judged by its cover!

The classroom provides a very interesting look at this behavior. I find it interesting that people will behave unprofessionally in the classroom and expect you to think they will operate like professionals in the 'real world.'

> Everything you say, everything you do, and everything you wear brands your company of One.

I have seen this play out many times in undergraduate engineering courses. The character a student displays in the classroom will carry forward and follow them. Their classmates and faculty have made a judgment of them and, without some powerful change of heart, that judgment will stick. Past students often ask me to be an employer reference for them, not realizing what they're asking for.

Remember, everything you say and do brands you! If you do not want your actions, words, and images played on the news tonight, do not offer them up to be replayed and repeated in the mind of someone who observes you during the day.

REALITY CHECK

Joe (named changed to protect the guilty) was a graduate student in my wireless communications class a few years ago. I really liked him, as did most people, but he clearly played the system, as he continuously looked for the shortcuts on projects, tests, even grades. He clearly intended to do the bare minimum.

Just a few months later, Joe was applying for a job with a company, and the CEO (who is a friend of mine) called to ask what I thought about Joe. While I liked Joe, I also liked the CEO and was not about to tell him that Joe was a stellar performer (which is what this CEO wanted to hear). He asked me, "Would you hire Joe?" I said, "no." That is all he needed to hear. Joe had branded himself as someone who wanted to do the least amount of work possible, and even after graduating with a Masters in Electrical Engineering, he was still wearing that brand.

SUGGESTIONS TO SUPERCHARGE YOUR COO

As COO, you should know your customers by now, and you should know what they want. So start delivering!

- **Greet them with a friendly smile.** It makes a *big* difference! Just think...they may be having a bad day, but being around you could make their day better. What better customer relations can you have? If you have a reputation for being a grouch, this will make an immediate impact!

- **Keep it positive.** Refuse to complain about others. Do not get dragged down into a gripe session. Walk away instead, or change the direction of the conversation, if you can. An ex-boss of mine named Jim was complaining to me about his boss, Julie. I reminded him that while Julie was not perfect, he knew what to expect from her. He thought about it and agreed—he *did* know what to expect from her. Knowing this, he began to prepare a message to approach her on a particular request. He started thinking about what *she* wanted to hear. In this simple reminder, I had turned his gripe session into a time where Jim became empowered. And I had avoided my own tendency to join in the griping session as well.

- **Look in the mirror.** What image are you presenting? The book, *Dress for Success,* was famous for saying you should dress for the job you want, not the job you have. I hate to admit it, but his book is right on target.

- **Take care of your production capacity.** As a Company of One, your greatest asset is your ability to work and to get to work. Are you taking care of your production capacity? Do you schedule routine maintenance for yourself including exercise, eating right, and plenty of sleep? What about your car? Are you just waiting for an emergency to throw you out of work? Create a plan and work it.

- **Get a clock.** Are you always late—rushing madly to every appointment? If so, your customers know it. Fix it. Learn a form of time management that works for you. I have worked with engineers who never showed up on time and rarely delivered on time. When they did show up, they had a long story of what had gone wrong and why they were late. They were a crisis-a-minute—brilliant engineers, but I would never work with them again. If this is you, find something that works. And if you are not sure if this is you or not, just ask your coworkers!

- **Be ahead of our customer.** Do you know that your customer needs something from you periodically, such as a statement or report? Then instead of waiting, deliver it to them ahead of time. A member of my team continually provides information I need even before I have realized that I need it. She is one step ahead of me. The good side is that she is not stressed by my demands—

she does the work on her own time, then puts the ball in my court.

- **Listen.** If you listen closely to your customers, you may discover things they need which they are not even aware of. Years ago I realized we needed a software application to track how time was being spent on various projects. Some co-workers and I developed a simple application in our spare time. Within months, our full-time jobs became application development—we had filled a true, yet previously unspoken, need.

- **How do you add value?** If you have not already done so, meet with your customers and learn how you add value. Listen to them!

- **Ask.** Ask your customers how you are performing and where you can improve in a way that would add the most value. Again, *listen*. Do not defend yourself, just listen.

- **Survey them.** Send a survey to your customers and your co-workers asking for honest feedback about your performance on some of your COO role activities. Even go high-tech and use a tool such as Survey Monkey on the web (which is free). A survey or written instrument tends to get better results because it shows others you really want serious feedback.

RELAX

OK, your mind should be spinning about things you can do...but you might be overwhelmed. Relax and prioritize. Get some balance. You need to think long term. Think about small things you can do and larger things you can begin to work on.

Start simple. For instance, if you do not exercise, start by taking a walk. If you are a grouch in the morning, try to smile when you are walking in the door, even if you have to fake it. The key is to get started and do *something*, then watch for the reaction from your customers! Nothing will motivate you and create momentum like some positive feedback from your customers. Take it a step at a time, but be intentional.

DEVELOP YOUR COMPANY OF ONE

Your job now, like many times before, is to brainstorm. Think about things you can do. Get a piece of paper out and just start writing ideas to improve your COO.

Look at the suggestions above. Some keys are:

1. Do the simple things. Look for easy ways to impact people. Greeting is the most obvious. Force yourself to be cheerful; it will become natural as you practice.

2. Be timely. Are there things you do regularly but your customer always has to ask you to do them? Schedule time to do those things sooner.

3. Add value. How can you not only do the things you normally do, but add a little more to them? Can you sort the report to make it easier to read? Can you provide a simple and short email to summarize major activities that you completed in the past week? Can you summarize a long written report in a simple half-page list of bullets?

4. Help prepare them. You know the meetings your customers are going into. Can you provide them with valuable data to make them look like super stars?

5. Volunteer. Is there something needing to be done that you can volunteer to do? It is often the unwanted projects that propel people to high levels of visibility.

7

CFO FOR YOUR COMPANY OF

ONE

"The main reason people struggle financially is because they have spent years in school but learned nothing about money. The result is that people learn to work for money .. but never learn to have money work for them." Robert Kiyosaki in Rich Dad Poor Dad [1]

Now let's look at the financial aspect of your company. For the average person, this is one of the most overlooked and mismanaged areas in our personal lives, despite the fact that there is no shortage of information in books, on websites, through articles and workshops, and other sources. Sure, some of the stuff out there is garbage and sorting out the good from the bad can be a bit of a challenge, but we do have a lot to work with. But this is like weight loss, exercise, and good eating habits—we know we need it, but it takes discipline to *make* it happen.

Typical Company	Company of One
Develop a budget	Develop a household budget
Pay bills	Pay bills
Manage cash and debt	Manage cash and debt
Conduct long-term financial planning	Plan for long-term financial goals
Fulfill legal reporting (IRS, etc.)	Fulfill legal reporting (IRS)
Manage risk	Manage risk of losses (insurance)
Do payroll	Manage risk due to inability to earn (disability insurance)
Secure records and set access to accounts	Secure privacy of records and set access to accounts
Make sure a profit is shown monthly	Make sure you have money at the end of the month, after paying bills
Provide annual financial reporting to owners	Provide periodic financial reporting to family
Measure performance! (ROI)	

Temptations to handle money poorly abound for us personally: credit is relatively easy to get; products are made more and more attractive and tempting; marketing machines convince us that we need and deserve what they have to offer. But, this is not true only for individuals—corporations face the same issues. Companies are bombarded daily by other companies wanting to sell them something that will solve their problems or create a 'better' image in the marketplace.

As you saw in the role of COO, most of these things should seem pretty obvious. Similar to what you saw earlier, in the table on the previous page you see a comparison between the CFO for a typical company and the CFO for your Company of One—notice that they are almost identical. The CFO is the person in charge of money and, like it or not, your Company of One uses money just like any other company.

Note that I am not telling you what action you should take—instead, I am suggesting to you *what education you need to get.* Since there is plenty of excellent information available to help any CFO, there is no need to repeat it all here. I am going to point you to excellent and easy-to-use resources you should really enjoy.

WHERE DO YOU STAND?

Looking at the table above, you are probably thinking that you are already doing a good deal of this work. But statistics indicate that many of you are not doing this very well. The first couple items on the list—budgeting, paying bills, filing taxes, etc.—you are certainly familiar with, even if you are not good at it. Most of us need more education in these basic skills—yes, even those of us who already have years of formal education. If you feel like you are the only one who does not understand money, be comforted in knowing that you are not alone. I have seen people who manage large groups and even lots of money at their jobs, but cannot seem to get a grip on their own household spending and planning.

WHAT DOES MY HOUSEHOLD BUDGET HAVE TO DO WITH MY COMPANY?

I get asked this all the time, so I think I need to be as clear as possible. Remember, your Company of One is *you*. Your income comes in, and your expenses go out. Your Company of One spends money on lots of things, including mortgages, food, entertainment, etc. Trying to separate your "business" income and expenses from your household expenses is meaningless. After all, the money you pay your mortgage with is the income from your Company of One.

In *Rich Dad Poor Dad*, Robert Kiyosaki shows how most people tend to spend their money on things that are expenses or liabilities. The more you consume, the more money it takes to pay for it all. Think of that boat, motorcycle, or other toy sitting in your driveway. You paid money for the toy and it continues to take money from you all the time in the form of personal property taxes, maintenance, insurance, etc. But Robert points out that the rich know they are a Company of One (he does not use that term, but it's the same idea) and they use their income more wisely. I will not go into the details here since he covers it well in his book.

So remember: you are a company. And if you are married with children, they are stakeholders of your Company of One. Sure, the analogy starts to break down here since corporations do not typically have families to support, yet, if you are married, you and your spouse are one, so he or she is part of your Company of One.

AM I INSECURE?

Take particular notice of the last two items on the list of CFO activities. Security has become a bigger issue with the advent of electronic banking and the growth of identity theft. While writing this chapter, I realized someone had taken one of my debit cards and charged four transactions totaling $1,000 in a single day. I do not check my accounts daily (well, I didn't then, anyway; now I do), so I just happened to catch them quickly.

Fortunately, my account was fixed and the bank refunded me the money. But what if I had less than $1,000 in the bank? What if it had been my only account? During the four or five days it took the bank to fix the account, I was essentially being held a financial hostage—I could do little with

> Security is one of the often-overlooked roles of the CFO.

that account. Had this been my main account, I am not sure the people I owed money to would have understood the delay. And trust me, my experience was minor. This happens to thousands of people every day, and may be happening to *you* right now.

Many of you have financial records on your computers including passwords that show how to get into your accounts. That might be OK if your computer is secured. Security is one of the often-overlooked roles of the CFO.

REPORT, PLEASE

Another key role of the CFO is reporting. Every owner needs to know how their investments are doing, and it is often in the hands of the CFO to report those results. Your Company of One is no different. If you are single and have no one depending on you, then you need to report to yourself. However, as I said before, if you are married and have children, the lives of others depend on your income and they need to get financial information on a regular basis.

Larry Burkett, founder of Crown Financial Ministries, wrote his wife a letter every year which contained details of what she would need to do to take over the finances if suddenly he were to become incapacitated. This is a great idea, and something I do with my wife.

Also, you and your family need to regularly get together to discuss finances, perhaps monthly. Having a budget that is written and can be discussed among adult family members is one way to get everyone on the same team. After all, in most families everyone spends money and in all families everyone depends on money.

In our case, Lea and I regularly discuss our bills and financial situation so we both understand where we are financially. This is part of my role as CFO.

MONEY IS FUEL

When I deal with venture capitalists, they talk about money being the fuel of companies. Money makes things happen and helps reach goals. A lack of money means the company ends up stranded on the sideline of the world of opportunity. They cannot reach their goals without fuel. In fact, they cannot do anything; they just fade away.

For our Company of One, money is fuel to help you reach your personal goals. What is your goal in relation to employment? Is it to provide for your family? To work toward retirement? To impact the world? Maybe it's all of the above? Like it or not, money is the key. Even if you are a person who is *not* driven by money and you do not define success in financial terms, you still must admit that money is important. Where money serves, nothing can take its place!

RICH DAD, POOR DAD

Robert Kiyosaki's book, *Rich Dad Poor Dad*, does a wonderful job spelling out the basics of how the wealthy look at money compared to the rest of the world. Even if your goal is not wealth, you need to know how to make money work for you, and you can learn this from seeing how the wealthy use their money.

Of key importance in his book is the idea of *where* we spend our money. Wealthy company owners spend their money buying assets (things that generate more money) like investments, real estate, businesses, and even books and courses to help them learn how to make money work for them. The rest of the world spends money on liabilities—defined as things that cost more and more money, like cars, TVs, boats, and even our expensive homes. We might need or enjoy some of these things, but the typical person spends much more on these items than they should—and that leaves little to nothing to buy assets.

BABY STEPS

If you find your Company of One in debt and having a difficult time controlling the money flow, then you need Dave Ramsey, the financial guru. Dave has a system of seven baby steps in his book, *Total Money Makeover*. These steps are guaranteed to break you free from debt and help you begin to build wealth.

The nice thing is that these seven steps are doable for normal people like you and me. They take discipline, but they're doable! The first is establishing a $1,000 emergency fund for a 'rainy day.' For many people, this emergency fund makes a world of difference and takes them out of the trap—it provides tons of freedom. Success is not dependent on how much you make. I know plenty of people making six-figure incomes who do not have the $1,000 cushion they need.

Dave's second step is getting yourself on a budget. All companies live and work on a budget, and so should your Company of One. Just these two steps will have a dramatic impact on your financial life, and can offer a great deal of peace!

DEVELOP YOUR COMPANY OF ONE

The CFO often needs education, or, to put that more accurately, he needs the *right* education. Let's take some real action! I know you are taking time to read this book right now, but I am suggesting *more* reading. Take heart, though, the books I am suggesting are easy reads— they're entertaining and even inspiring! Trust me; I am not a reader, but I have read these books cover-to-cover with ease.

- **Review Dave Ramsey's baby steps.** I suggest buying his book and even going to his training, if you can. To get started, simply get familiar with the system. Evaluate your current situation-- which step are you on? Then plan to attend his class. You can find these steps at http://www.daveramsey.com/new/baby-steps.

- **Read *Rich Dad Poor Dad.*** But first, just read pages 55-81. Reflect on how you are using your cash flow. Then take time to read the rest of the book.

- **Make records.** Make a record of all your accounts and passwords and put them in a safe place. Learn about security issues and how to best secure your data.

- **Set strong passwords.** Forget the birthday or address passwords—create *strong* passwords. Most financial institutions are forcing strong passwords today, but you also need to have a secure means of keeping up with them. You can buy programs that will store them in an encrypted file, but if you lose your hard drive, you may be toast. So you also need to backup your files! I use a tool called SplashID to track and encrypt my passwords and logins. There are many other password management programs on the market. If you choose to keep a list of passwords, these tools are a good bet.

- **Back up your files.** We use Carbonite to provide secure online backup that we can access anytime, even if our computers crash. Consider some type of backup for your personal data that will keep your financial records, your photos, etc., off-site in case your house burns down or gets flooded. The more automatic your backup method, the better. I do a monthly check to make sure the data is backed up, but for the most part, it happens without my noticing.

- **Secure your premises.** If you have a lot of data on your computer, password-protect it. Do not let friends or children access your computer and your files. Some may decide to take a peek while others will accidently share them with the world via a virus or hacker they have unwittingly allowed in. We have computers in our home that store financial data, however, we do not allow the kids or guests to use those computers.

- **Become educated on identity theft.** Dave Ramsey's book will walk you though some basics, but you also might want to get a service such as LifeLock to help watch all your data out there. I am not endorsing LifeLock or any other particular identity theft service company, but looking at your options is a wise investment of time. Identity theft protection is insurance against risk, and the risk is real.

8

CRO FOR YOUR COMPANY OF

ONE

"Telling the future by looking at the past assumes that conditions remain constant. This is like driving a car by looking in the rearview mirror." Herb Brody[1]

Most companies do not really have a position called "research officer." This role—to watch the future—is often divided among many people who collectively help guard the future of the company by keeping watch over the industry and economic environment. What are they watching for? Everything is in play here: new technologies, market changes, political decisions, trade among countries, war, and sometimes even weather patterns.

The chart below gives you another comparison of roles so you can examine how the CRO for your Company of One is performing:

Typical Company	Company of One
Consider how to evaluate and/or test possible innovations	Ask continuously: What will you be selling in the future? What are the markets doing with your current service offerings? Are they at risk?
Keep up with industry news and trends by reading	Ask constantly, "What do I need to know to get to where I want to go?"
Learn new management and/or leadership techniques	Read in your field
Learn better means of serving customers	Become better educated about how to run your company
Keep up by talking to vendors	Consider better methods to serve your customer
Seek new sources of quality information continually	Consider better methods to communicate with the customer
Look continuously for better ways to serve the customer, deliver the goods, interface with the customer, improve performance, add value, and save money. Sometimes these are technology changes, but in reality they're mainly processes and products. These include short-term projects as well as long-term projects.	Seek new sources of quality information continually

We can break the CRO role into two domains: short-term and long-term. The short-term role is concerned about what is happening now and over the next year. What can be done quickly to be more efficient or provide better service for our customers? While technology might be a key factor here, it is not the driving issue. Efficiency and service are often a matter of process, not technology. Technology is simply a set of tools to help the processes.

In the long-term role, the CRO should keep an eye on trends. How will politics, markets, technology, etc. impact their company's market? Think about a railroad tycoon in the early 1900's—if they had not been paying attention, the advent of the automobile could have completely changed their fortune—almost overnight. Then consider more recent events like hurricanes, oil spills, and real estate markets on the Gulf Coast—many companies have been damaged or driven out of business by these changes.

ONE-YEAR FOCUS

The first role of the CRO is to look at process improvement. How can your Company of One get better results? As CRO, you must interact with your other roles to determine what is important and where you need to spend your time and money. What should you outsource or eliminate? For example, I have recently hired someone to cut my grass. This simple change has provided me more time to do what I want (and mowing the yard was never very high on my list of favored activities). Also, I sold my riding mower, because it was just one more thing costing me money and taking up room.

Another small change I made involved my computer backups: I bought Carbonite as a means to continually backup my systems offline. Here my internal CFO and CRO worked together. Again, a small thing that, while important, was not something I wanted to hassle with on a regular basis. In my companies, I have also outsourced newsletter writing, customer service, and shipping. These tasks are being done better than I was doing them and I have more time for other tasks. Now I have to follow up and make sure the processes are being run the way I want.

For your one-year focus, you need to look at your roles, then determine what matters most and what you can do best. Things which are important, but are not your expertise, need to be outsourced to others, or you need to get educated so you can do them yourself. Things that matter less need to be eliminated, delegated, or outsourced. You need to focus your time and energy on the things that really matter and where your Company of One adds real value to your customers.

Patrick Cash, a friend of mine who owns an Internet marketing company, recently told me he had outsourced his entire fulfillment operation. Previously, when he got an order for his educational DVDs, he would burn the DVD and ship it. Over time he started having the DVDs mass produced and hired a friend of his to ship them. Now he has automated the entire process and he does not touch the product—third-party companies do it all. His job is marketing the products and finding new things to sell. This is key since Patrick's special skill is marketing, not shipping. He now has more time to make more money, and is paying a small fee to have the rest of the work done by others.

THE LONG VIEW

What is happening to your work? What is the market thinking about the one key thing you sell? Take a software developer for example. Not so many years ago the software developer was a highly skilled and highly valued individual. Now, many software developer roles are strictly a commodity—something bought at discounted prices from anywhere in the world at any time. If the developer was not watching his or her market, they would suddenly find themselves undervalued and out of work. Many have done just that. What if you are a project manager for a large healthcare company? Could your employer outsource all project management work to a consulting company? Sure they could, and many already have.

Your CRO needs to be thinking about these things and helping to direct your Company of One to take action. You can fight the changes, but there is no point. You will be better served by positioning yourself for the future. For instance, if you are a software developer, can you start the outsourcing process yourself and show your employer that you can triple your capacity by managing multiple outsourced projects rather than writing the code yourself? Your "secret sauce" might be interfacing with customers and finding their needs, not coding.

Think about companies in the video rental business. A few years ago, these companies were rolling in cash. But now they are dying fast as the media of choice is becoming online delivery, not DVD. The record companies fought for years against downloadable music, but it was a losing battle. Now Apple has made deals with the recording companies to provide most music in a downloadable format for a fraction of the price via iTunes.

And consider where I am. I work for a large university. People around me see the university model as working forever. After all, everyone needs a college degree, right? Yet, as the cost of college is rising and the return on investment (ROI) is decreasing, students and their parents are starting to question the model. Is college really needed? Is there another way to get a good education? The number of people asking such questions are few today, but that could change overnight and the university must be ready to respond.

With tools like the Internet, we can all get an education free of charge! A motivated student could get the equivalent of a degree from MIT without ever spending a dime at the university. What happens when employers start to value this form of education as much as that earned inside the walls of brick-and-mortar buildings? I would suggest many employers already have, yet a lot of people in higher education have stuck their heads in the sand. The smart ones are looking at what the customer wants (yes, the student is the customer) and are beginning to consider how to deliver better results. In my view, the university of the near future will look much different than what we see today.

Where is your Company of One going? Are you fighting the change that is bound to come? Or are you stuck with your head in the sand pretending all is well? If so, your CRO needs to get busy!

EDUCATION IS KEY

As CRO, you must be educating yourself continuously. I have no issue with education, but it must be the *right* education. If your Company of One is moving toward becoming software development engineer, then you could go back to University XYZ and get a degree (or a second degree) in computer science. But would it make more sense to learn from people who run companies like the one you want to create? Are there courses on the market that teach you how to be a software consultant? (The answer is yes!) You might do better with a short course—paying a few thousand dollars—rather than investing years on a college degree that might not result in any ROI. Again, the *right* education is the key. As CRO, you need to know where your Company of One is going and get the right education to prepare for the future.

SWOT YOURSELF

A favorite tool for consultants and MBA courses is the SWOT, or **S**trengths, **W**eaknesses, **O**pportunities, and **T**hreats. Your CRO should make such a list.

Strengths: What are your strengths? What sets you apart from your competition?

Weaknesses: What about your weaknesses?

Be honest here and write down what is real. Do not think you are strong at software development just because that is your job title. When I was a software developer, I felt I always had to be the best, yet I knew I could never compete with those people who seemed to live and breathe software development. They were good; I was mediocre at best.

I really struggled with an identity crisis here. I was really great at defining customer requirements and helping clients and customers integrate systems into their work. When I looked honestly at myself, I realized I had true strengths related to my work, but writing code was not one of them.

How about you? Where are you truly strong and where are you truly weak? When I realized I had strengths, I was able to work with the code developers while I became the customer connection—a much better situation for all involved.

Opportunities: What opportunities do you have? What could you do easily to take advantage of them?

Threats: What is lurking beneath the surface? What changes are on the horizon for you and your company?

A common threat to all of us who depend on a single company to provide all the income for our Company of One is losing that one customer. It could happen at any time and for any reason. But, more important, our entire service offering could be at risk. Technology and societal changes might threaten the very existence of your Company of One.

How easy can what you offer be outsourced or automated? Is a trend developing in that direction? Is there an opportunity in those trends? The person responsible for quality assurance for a telecom company might find that the entire role is taking on new meaning and is being outsourced and automated. Yet, they might be able to rise above their position and realize that someone needs to be the interface between the outsourced or automated process and the customer who is measuring quality. You might be able to transfer your skills into this new opportunity, and possibly offer consulting services.

A SWOT analysis is simply a brainstorming process of writing down a lot of things that are obvious, some that are not so obvious, and looking at a clear picture of your situation.

DEVELOP YOUR COMPANY OF ONE

The CRO role is one we often neglect out of fear. We tend to put our head down and continue to work, looking for pay raises and better jobs, but rarely looking around to see the brutal truths. Instead of reacting out of fear, you need to take responsibility and consider your choices so you can choose how your Company of One will respond to change.

- **SWOT.** Develop a SWOT list for your Company of One. What obvious actions might you take as a result of your list?

- **Short-term fixes.** If you are doing your work in the other roles, you should already know what your customers really value and what is less important to them. What can you eliminate? What can you delegate to others? What can you outsource to others? How can you improve your ability to produce more and at a higher level of quality?

- **Get the pulse.** What can you do to stay on top of the pulse of your industry? Are there trade shows or meetings you need to be attending? Publications you should be reading? Find out how to be 'in the know' rather than in the dark, then take action to become enlightened.

- **Confront the brutal fears.** Write down what is happening already or what you fear may happen with your current method of income generation. If you fear it, deal with the reality of the fear.

- **Ask.** Seek the obvious predictions for your career. Ask yourself: how might your customers get the same services you are performing for them from other people at a lower price? Or perhaps what you are doing is quickly becoming a thing of the past. Be honest and ask for feedback from your customers and industry experts.

- **Confront the brutal facts.** Now deal with the facts. Write down the real threats to your current source of income.

- **Seek opportunities.** This is the exciting part! How might you counter the threats you identified? How can you turn a threat into an opportunity? Think about the possibilities!

9

CMO FOR YOUR COMPANY OF

ONE

"...while you're looking at other [greener] pastures, other people are looking at yours." Earl Nightingale ¹

The CMO is another role that not every company will have formally defined. But, you can bet this role is a *serious* deal. Corporations all over the world, of all sizes, spend masses of money on marketing. Some of that money is a good investment; some is wasted because the marketing ended up creating little impact on the company's bottom line.

Yet it is in the marketing effort that we all form our opinions of companies—at least our initial opinions. The image that comes to mind when I mention organizations like Microsoft, Apple, Coke, CNN, and even the US Marines is no accident—it was painstakingly planned and developed by marketing people.

Below you'll find another comparison between a typical company and your Company of One. Read these closely and let it really sink in!

Typical Company	Company of One
Create and manage company brand	Create and manage your brand
Bring in money via sales	Generate the flow of money via the sale of services
Develop marketing materials	Develop marketing materials
Defend brand	Defend brand
Study market for changing demands and new product ideas	Study market for changing demands and new ways to make money
Get continual feedback on customer satisfaction	Get continual feedback on customer satisfaction
Counter buyer's remorse by creating means of reminding customer of value	Deal with buyer's remorse by continually showing customers how you add value
Work to create customer loyalty	Stay in constant contact with customer to develop a strong bond of loyalty
Network with customers, vendors, related industries, and competitors to keep connected and find new opportunities	Do intentional and strategic networking to help identify new opportunities and stay connected
Participate in and provide leadership for outside activities that add value to others such as roles with professional associations, community groups, and charitable organizations	Become known for adding value by serving in professional, community, or charitable organizations

This kind of marketing is what you need to do for your Company of One. No, you cannot simply let your work speak for itself. *Why not?* Because few people experience your work firsthand, but your entire market (and beyond) can form an image of you and your company.

Think of it this way: not everyone owns a Rolex, but we all have an image of that company and its products, don't we? The same goes for Leer Jet, Ritz Carlton, Motel 8, Neiman Marcus, Kmart, even Google. We have in our minds an idea of what the company offers and the quality of their products, even if we have never experienced their products firsthand. So, if you're content to let your work speak for itself, there will be very few people listening.

The other roles of your company may have seemed pretty straightforward, but hang on for this one. The areas of the CMO and CEO are usually the most neglected areas of any Company of One, yet these two areas are very critical—perhaps the most critical in order for you to have a strategic plan for your career and life!

Let's spend a few minutes looking at this in detail. I will cover networking in a later chapter since it needs special attention.

DO YOU KNOW WHAT YOUR BRAND IS?

Like a brand on cattle, a marketing brand identifies a specific product, service, or company. Just hearing the words of the brand such as IBM, Coca-Cola, or Apple, you get a particular image in your mind. When you hear "it's the real thing" you may immediately think of Coca-Cola.

Remembering the company or the product is not the key—it's *how* you remember the company or the product's relationship to you that matters. You may remember comical advertisements, catchy slogans, or striking color combinations that remind you of a company's image. If you walk into an Apple store, the clean sleek stainless steel image will never leave you—it effectively brands who they are, for better or worse. If you have ever had a bad relationship with Apple, that brand image would conjure up negative feelings. Think about how you feel when you see the name or face of a politician you strongly dislike. That is branding...in a bad way.

What is *your* brand? When people hear your name, what images or thoughts come to their minds? I'm not talking here about your friends and family (who I hope see you in a positive light), but about your coworkers, employers, and employees...people you have identified as customers. How do *they* see you? What impressions have you left with them? Do people know you as the slacker who tries to get out of work or constantly complains, like the bitter pill I mentioned earlier? Or when they hear your name do they remember the person who delivers as promised and keeps commitments?

What is your brand? And what would you *like* it to be?

Think about who, in your office, comes to mind when I ask these things:

Who do you go to when you need to 'get it done'?

Who do you get honest answers from?

Who tells you what you want to hear but is often lying?

Who do you need to follow up with to make sure they actually did what they promised or were assigned?

Who do you want to avoid because they are a bitter pill?

Who will talk endlessly about nothing and waste your time?

Who is most likely to be looking at pornography?

Who will tell you a dirty joke?

Can you think of a name for each of these? If so, that is their brand. What is yours?

How do you find out what your brand is? *Ask!* Yes, I am serious—just ask. I have done this recently. I sent an email to a few key customers asking them to rate my leadership ability. The feedback was honest and very useful. It is amazing what people will tell you when they know that you're really trying to improve yourself. Here is how I would ask in an email:

> *I am working on some personal exercises in the book, "Resumes are Worthless." The author suggests I ask for feedback from peers, coworkers, and bosses about how I am perceived by others. So I am asking you for honest feedback and/or constructive criticism. This request is an attempt to improve my performance and service to each of you, so please give me the hard truth.*

If you send an email like this, you might even give them some specifics. For example, you might ask them to rate you on a scale of one to five (with five being best) on the following criteria:

o   Friendliness
o   Open to new ideas
o   Easy to work with
o   Ability to deliver results
o   Innovative thinking
o   Leadership

Add to this list as needed, but keep it short enough that people will actually respond to you. A maximum of 10 criteria should provide you with ample feedback.

If this whole exercise scares you, *good*! If you think you have a terrible brand, then don't be fearful and hesitate, go ahead and ask. Note that simply by asking, you improve your

What is your brand? When people hear your name, what images or thoughts come to their minds?

brand! Let me say that again: *just by asking you improve your brand.* People will not see this request as a negative, but as a positive. They will see this as an attempt to improve yourself. You will appear to actually care and you will make them question their own brand!

You might choose to get feedback in other ways, and that is OK. But you *do* need to get feedback. Be sure to ask people you barely know or rarely work with. Why? Because people talk. Asking for feedback from someone in another department or division will help you determine what the rumor mill has been saying about you. After all, I am sure you have formed opinions about people who work in other areas of your organization, haven't you?

However you ask for feedback, be careful not to react to it when it arrives. Do not defend yourself or attack the messenger! Do not ask for reasons behind their feedback. Just say, "thank you for your feedback" and evaluate the results alone or with a close friend. Looking at the results, where are you strong and where are you weak? Where is your perception of yourself way off from how others see you?

What if your brand is terrible? What if people seem to hate working with you? Take heart—brands can be fixed! Companies do it all the time. First you have to know the brutal truth, then you can take action towards improving.

As I write this, Toyota is coming off a long line of recalls and negative publicity about their brakes and sticking gas pedals. Their advertisements show a company that realizes the serious issues they have and is deeply committed to resolving the problems. They are showing honesty and openness. If they continue the path and fix the problems, their brand will recover.

The same goes for BP, who, over the summer of 2010, was dumping oil into the Gulf of Mexico from a busted well. You may think they will never recover a positive brand image, but my bet is that they will. Their marketing and PR efforts are already having an effect on the perception of their company by showing they really care about the impact of the problem and they want to resolve their mess. If the message is honest, it will work. It may take years, but it will work.

The same goes for you! If you have negative feedback, you can start taking action now to show you care about the results. You can talk honestly with others about how you were rated and make it known that you want to improve. Others will be watching, but in general, everyone will want the best for you and they will help you!

If you have wonderful feedback, view the results with a little caution to be sure you have asked the right questions and are not getting false accolades. But if it is real, the comments you got may be a great indicator of the services your customer really values. For instance, if they make comments to you about how you always deliver on time, this is a clue that they value timely service. But to keep from being fooled, keep a keen ear out and keep asking.

WHAT'S IN AN AD?

Next, let's consider your advertising. What? Did I say your *advertising*? Yes, I did. Are you under the impression that you do not advertise? Do you think you don't *need* to advertise? You are very wrong! Coca-Cola is one of the best-known products and brands worldwide, yet they advertise constantly. Why? They do not want us to forget that they are "the real thing." If they let up for a moment, they will find that Pepsi is the "best thing" and the new "real thing." Someone is on their heels chasing them, wanting to take their position in the market as their own.

Well, guess what—you are no different. Someone out there wants your job. Someone wants your position and status. Even if you do not think you have anything worth taking, someone else wants it! Earl Nightingale states in his book, *Lead the Field,* that "while you're looking at other [greener] pastures, other people are looking at yours."

So how are you advertising? How are you reminding those around you that *you* are the one who gets the job done? How are you reminding those who pay your salary that you are worth every penny and more? Do you think they know? Do you think they remember? *Don't count on it!*

Now I know what you're thinking: "Is this nut suggesting I take out ads in magazines? Is he suggesting I buy TV time?" Well, probably not. The key to advertising is that you have to get the message to *your* customers.

Coca-Cola advertises to specific groups of people in their ads. The ads they place on American Idol are geared to reach that specific group of customers. (Have you seen them? Watch closely.) Plus, by being on a TV show with a large audience, they reach many customers at one time. You have to find ways to get in front of your customers and those you want to *become* your customers! Who do you want to know and appreciate your brand?

WHAT IS YOUR RESUME SELLING?

Have you ever studied a TV commercial closely? Instead of running off to refresh your drink, watch them. What are they advertising? What is their message? Are they selling you the benefits of the product or are they selling you its features? Features are part of the product and benefits are what the product does for the customer.

Think about a TV commercial for an automobile. The features are characteristics of the product, such as how many doors it has or the engine size. Benefits are advantages of the product which impact the customer, such as how driving a particular car might make the owner feel 'macho', smart, economical, sophisticated, or young. Benefits improve the customer's position, feelings, view of themselves, happiness, safety, etc. I think you will see, more often than not, that ads are selling benefits.

> Someone out there wants your job. Someone wants your position and status. Even if you do not think you have anything worth taking, someone else wants it!

Why do you care what a TV or magazine ad sells? What does this have to do with *you*? Everything! Most companies that place television ads are spending millions of dollars on advertising and, like them or not, they know what works and why. These guys are the pros at communicating a message and they know what works. Remember those car sales TV commercials? The salesmen are always yelling at you, right? Do you know why? Because it works!

What about *your* ads? In fact, what ads do you even have? For most of us we have one advertisement: our resume. What does it say? Here is a commonly suggested outline for a resume:

NAME / CONTACT INFORMATION

OBJECTIVE

EDUCATION

EXPERIENCE

SKILLS

HONORS & AWARDS

ACTIVITIES/SPECIAL INTERESTS

REFERENCES

One of the things I often notice on resumes is an Objective, which states something like, "I want to make a lot of money." OK, perhaps that is not what yours says, but that is what the employer reads. Think about it. What does the employer care about *your* objective?

When I interview someone and they show me their resume (let me be in full disclosure: I hate resumes!) I look for the objective. Then I love to ask, "Why do you think I care about your objective?" This question startles them. I then point out that I only care about *my* objectives. What they should be selling me is how they can help *me* reach *mine!*

Again, think TV commercials. What if the CEO of Ford were to show up on your television tonight saying, "we have decided that we want to make twice as much money this year as last, so we can buy some new jets and redecorate our offices, so please buy a Ford." Would that inspire you to go buy a Ford? This may actually be their objective, but Ford knows the simple truth of business: customers don't care what Ford's objective is, they care about their own.

So look at your resume. Put yourself in the position of the person reading it. What do *they* care about? Not your objectives. Not your degrees. When they read your resume, what they have in mind are two things:

What help do they need, and can you deliver it?

Do they have any connections to you?

First, consider the help they need. Companies do not hire people unless they have a pain or desire they want to resolve. When you hire someone to mow your yard, it is because you want your yard to look a certain way, but you do not want to go to the pain to mow it yourself. You do not hire that company because their objective is to become the largest lawn care service in the city, do you?

Or, someone might want to hire a professional because they possess a special expertise. You might hire a decorator because you want your house to be a great showplace and you know that a specific decorator can deliver that desired image.

Everything you say and do brands your company of One.

In business, we hire for the same reasons: we have a pain. We have customers to take care of, reports to write, inventory to manage, etc. We do not want to do the work ourselves, so we hire someone. Or, perhaps we are trying to grow our company by offering stunning support to our customers. Then we want to hire support people who have a specific expertise—people we know can fulfill our desires. How does your resume reflect these needed benefits? Put yourself in the hiring manager's shoes and think about how your resume addresses their needs.

Secondly, a resume might make a connection between you and a hiring manager (your potential customer)—and this is valuable. This is why BP featured a local New Orleans man in their advertisements, saying he lives in the city and works for BP. He made a connection to the people. BP's message was, "we are just like you and we care, too."

In the same way, your resume may make a connection with the hiring manager who reads it. Your resume might mention your Cub Scout leadership activities. It may be insignificant in relation to the job, but the hiring manager might highly value Cub Scouts! You just made a connection—and more often than you think, this kind of connection sells!

To accomplish your business objectives, you must sell others on the benefits you can bring to them through your products and services.

So revisit your resume. List all possible connections including schools, fraternities/sororities, volunteer work, etc. But focus the majority of your attention on the benefits you offer to the company. I suggest that you craft your resume more like an ad, but popular resume philosophy is against that. So, instead, keep the resume and just write it with the reader in mind.

OTHER ADS?

Now the scary thing to me is that most of you have only one specific ad—your resume. And, once you're hired, no one will care about it again. What *other* information are you sending to remind your customers or potential customers what you do, have done, or can do? I am sure you have sent some—the question is whether you have controlled the message. Consider your emails, your voicemails, and sticky notes left on colleagues' desks.

Company leaders know that everything you say and do brands the company. Think about it! We have all seen politicians make a stupid gaffe that brands him or her for years. Think about BP's former CEO,

Tony Hayward, who was seen sailing the day after he testified before Congress. Fair or not, this brands him and BP. Shortly afterward, he was relieved of his duties as CEO.

What messages do you convey? Look at your emails: are they sloppy and unprofessional or do they spew complaints? What do they truly communicate? Is it:

"I am a go-getter who gets results" or

"I am a complainer" or

"I want to do the least I can and still get paid"?

What about your workspace? What does it say about you? What about your voicemail? Years ago, I overheard a coworker leaving a voicemail for someone. He kept saying the same message over and over, as if he were practicing a speech. I heard him leave the message, then silence for a minute, and then he would say it again.

I went into his office to see if he had gone nuts. He told me he always listened to the messages he left and if he did not like them he re-recorded them. He said to me, "Everything I say and do brands me, so when I have a chance to get it right, I take it."

In this same way, you need to consider *your* messages and how *you* communicate the value you provide. Are the people reading the reports you write aware that *you* wrote them? Do your contributions in meetings go unnoticed and unknown? *Does your boss even know what you are doing?* Many people in the corporate chaos today are lost in the crowd and even their bosses are clueless about the contributions they are making.

BUYER'S REMORSE

I mentioned buyer's remorse in a previous chapter. Let's revisit that for a moment. Have you ever bought something expensive and then later regretted it? Did you later think that you really should not have spent that much money? Just the other day I had a flat tire on my car and it could not be repaired.

Before I got out of the shop I had spent $490 on two new tires and a front-end alignment. I drove away thinking I had been taken. In reality, I had resolved issues that needed to be addressed, but the feeling of remorse still took over.

Buyer's remorse is a powerful emotion and one that really must be dealt with if you want to protect your brand. Ever buy a new car? Usually you will get a letter or call from the dealer to thank you and remind you of the great deal and great value you have gotten. They are dealing with the potential of buyer's remorse and are trying to move you to feelings of pride about your purchase. Buyer's remorse tends to come soon after the money has been paid, but then goes away, so they know to contact you during this important time.

> *Are you dealing with the buyer's remorse your employer feels? When was the last time you made it clear that you bring value to the company?*

But your employer pays you every two weeks or month, right? Do they have remorse over writing that check? Let me speak as an employer: the answer is *yes*. Are you dealing with the buyer's remorse your employer feels? When was the last time you made it clear that you bring value to the company? Or, to put it more directly, "what have you done for them lately?"

You might find the same thing, and if this is the case, it should cause you great concern. Someone in the company knows what is important, and if your leader is not that person, you might find yourself led to the unemployment line!

REALITY CHECK

The problem with buyer's remorse and your advertising is that you need to understand the benefits you provide. You must discover what your customers consider important and learn about the value you provide for them.

Recently a group of people I was working with did just this. They were given the following assignment to evaluate how their Company of One was providing services to their current employer:

Clearly define your list of customers by writing them down by name and by position. How do they impact your Company of One? Are they able to fire you? Are they a key to getting more money? Are they a key contributor to your reputation? Be careful not to judge too quickly—look carefully!

- What are the key results your customers expect from you? Actually ask them.

- How do your *key* customers measure your value? Ask them how they measure results in the key areas they defined in the previous question.

- If you could double your performance, could you double your salary? (*Ask!*)

- What business are you in today? What are you paid to do?

Most of the people in this group worked for large companies. While a few got very clear answers and learned things they did not expect, many were told that they would have a review later and these issues would be covered then. When I asked the group what they thought that answer meant, they all concluded that their boss did not know what was important, so he or she could not discuss it.

HOW DO I ADD VALUE?

To understand how to demonstrate your benefits, you first need to know what benefits your customers desire. See the assignment I gave the group in the *Reality Check* and try it yourself. You *must* know what is important to your customers! *You must!*

DOUBLE YOUR SALARY?

I learned to ask this question from the book, *Eat that Frog!*, by Brian Tracy. Brian suggests that you first learn what is most important to your employer. What three things that you do add the most value to the company? Ask your employer if they will help you delegate or eliminate less important activities.

If they agree, then ask, "If I can double the output on the items that add the most value, would you double my salary?"

I posed this scenario to a group of corporate people the other day. You could feel the air being sucked out of the room as they all seemed to gasp in unison. Then, in an uproar, several started to explain:

> *You cannot ask that in a major corporation.*

> *My boss does not have control over salaries.*

> *Our organization has pre-set levels, so that is not a valid question.*

A few people in the group even told me that if their employees asked such a question, they would fire them! Odd? When I ask successful entrepreneurs what they would do if asked this question they say, "we would love to have people ask us this question! We want results, and people focused on getting results is what matters most!"

This *is* a fair question. After all, if you were mowing lawns for a living and you could mow twice as many in a day, you would expect to make twice as much money. And, I suspect that most of you are working for money, right? So if you gave your employer twice the output by focusing on what was important, then you would expect twice the pay. That just makes sense.

I have seen people ask this question and get real results. Sure, your pay grade might not allow a doubling of your salary, but guess what...there are a lot of pay grades out there! If you were the CEO or President of a company, this link between pay and performance is not only a fair question, it is expected!

If you are not comfortable asking this question, then consider the question. If you cannot ask without the threat of getting fired, you might be with the wrong company. Your Company of One should have the ability to control its income just like other companies do.

KEEP IT COMING

I cannot stress enough that most people do a *terrible* job of marketing themselves. But I also cannot stress enough just how important this is! If you think marketing is slimy and not for you, then you are missing the point. I am not talking about selling used cars, but about keeping in touch with your customers and knowing how you are adding value to them. Isn't that why you are working?

> Don't we all want to add value to others and have a purpose? Don't you want others to rely on and value your service? I think you do.

So you need to continually be asking about and looking at how you impact others. Periodically you need to remind your customers of the value you provide. Do not wait for things like required monthly reports which, likely, are never read. Instead, find ways to *show* your customers how you add value.

Send an email once a month with a short, bulleted list outlining your recent accomplishments. Send them a thank-you card noting what you have done and asking if you are on target. Send them a survey that asks questions about how they would rate your service in a particular area—this has the dual benefit of getting feedback *and* reminding them of what you do! Be creative and do what works in your situation...but *do something!*

> *Periodically you need to remind your customers of the value you provide. . .find ways to show your customers how you add value.*

NETWORKING

One thing we have not considered in this section is networking. In the CMO chart, you see networking as a key element. But I am going to wait to cover that in a later chapter, after we look at the CEO's role—the reasons will be evident. First, we need to look at the CEO, which holds the real strategic view of your Company of One.

DEVELOP YOUR COMPANY OF ONE

The CMO role is perhaps the most overlooked role of the Company of One. In this chapter, we have explored some of the issues: knowing your customer and your brand.

All successful companies know that marketing is key. In fact, many might say that marketing and sales are the most important roles in any company. You need to make sure your Company of One does it well. Let's take some real action!

1. Ask for feedback from your customers and others about your brand. Find out how you are perceived. Remember not to take it personally or defend yourself, just thank them for their honest feedback.

2. What business are you in? What are you paid to do?

3. Clearly define your list of customers by writing them down by name and by position. How do they impact your Company of One? Are they able to fire you? Are they a key to getting more money? Are they a key contributor to your reputation? Be careful not to judge too quickly! Look carefully.

4. What are the key results your customers expect from you? Ask them!

5. How do your key customers measure your value? Ask!

10

CEO FOR YOUR COMPANY OF

ONE

"Most of us lead our lives like racehorses giving pony rides."
Dale Callahan

You have been through a lot. You have looked at a lot of the internal roles for your Company of One. Are you asking the key question yet? You know what it is: "What if my current job is not what I want to do?"

The fact is that, for most of you, your current job is *not* the right fit for you. Let me go further: for most of you, your current job is slowly sucking the life out of you. Yet, it is putting food on the table. You've heard all the advice, "just take a leap and go and do what you love. Live your dream! Chase your passion." I agree, but I think most people who give this advice are living in fantasyland.

Most of you have responsibilities—in particular, a family. As a Christian I believe this statement:

"But if anyone does not provide for his relatives, and especially for members of his household, he has denied the faith and is worse than an unbeliever." 1 Timothy 5:8 (English Standard Version)

Even if you are not a Christian, I think the sentiment of this statement should resonate well in your heart. We all hear about those people who risked it all and won big. But believe me, there are many more who have risked it all and lost even bigger. I figure God gave us brains, and *we should use them!*

CASH COW

Let's put this in perspective. Today, you may not be doing what you love, but it *does* bring in money. For most of you, making a change to work you would love doing is not that easy.

First, let's think about a traditional company. Very often a company is in the process of changing directions while their current business is still operating and making money. They know what has worked well in their business, they have a reputation, and keeping the money flowing in is relatively easy. We call that line of business the "cash cow." Just like a cow that keeps giving milk, a cash cow for our company keeps providing income.

For example, let us assume that right now the board of directors for WalMart is meeting to talk about their future. They have decided to go into the automotive manufacturing business. Although this is a major change for the company's direction, they see huge

For you, your cash cow is your current job or career.

opportunity in developing cars that are truly American-made and affordable to everyone. Their board might also see that their brick-and-mortar store has a lifespan that is coming to an end. They may be convinced that online retailers like Amazon are going to take over physical retail stores. So, for all the reasons above, they move into automotive.

This is a big leap. To make it happen will take a lot of work in R&D as well as marketing and manufacturing the initial products. The board decides that it will take three years to go to market with their first cars. While they are working on the cars in the background, their "cash cow" retail stores will continue to pay the bills and fund their future.

For you, your cash cow is your current job or career. For instance, a good friend of mine is a technical expert who supports enterprise systems. This is his cash cow. He knows the business and is very good at it, but he also knows that his particular role is dying off and will come to an end in the near future. His passion is teaching. What he would like to do next is teach full-time in a college university or become a professional trainer. Like WalMart, he has a cash cow and it is funding his transition.

REALITY CHECK

I recently received this email from a client in our graduate program at UAB. This email states very well the feelings I hear expressed by so many people in corporate America:

> "Since I began this program, I have been really thinking about my current employment situation and many concerns have been raised. If I view my position as a business and not just as a job, my business is at great risk.

> I have a long-term contract with one client that is renewed each year. The client is a large manufacturer that is doing well but they are in a struggling industry. The dynamics of the company are changing to adjust to the economy and I have been trying to see where I fit in. I have recently realized that I'm not a part of those dynamics. I am a supplier of a service that can easily be eliminated or replaced. My position requires a certain

level of business acumen but does not necessarily require a unique skill-set.

I work a full-time schedule and am bound by the same rules as a full-time employee, but I do not share the benefits that employees get. My position does not allow the time or flexibility to work with any other clients and the plant is located far away from other businesses. I can only reasonably work with this one client on any given day.

I have become aware that I am the only one that is at risk in this equation and the risk is great. I am a company of one, with one client and no real agent to look out for my best interests. I feel that if I'm taking all of the risk, I should receive all of the reward, but here it doesn't work that way. I enjoy working in this field and I'm not on the verge of quitting my job today, but I feel that change is needed. "

Does this sound familiar? There are probably many people who could read that write-up and say, "me too." My initial response to this message is to congratulate him on being able to honestly assess his situation. A lot of people are blinded to the "Company of One" thinking and they fool themselves into thinking all is OK. The truth may hurt, but being aware of it helps you look at what you really need to do. So I am suggesting that he has taken a great big step already, but...

What I see missing are some even bigger questions: What do you *really* want? Where do you *really* want to be? Certainly you could improve on your situation and do many things to get more control, but the reality is that it will take work and time—and if you are not going after what you really want, you're wasting time!

THE CEO'S ROLE

Now the question to ask is, "What is your transition plan?" Do you know where you want to go? Do you know what you want to do? Even if you like your current job and career, are you at risk like the guy in the *Reality Check*?

We have been looking at roles that are involved with the internal operation of the company, but the CEO has a dual role. First, the CEO tries to keep the whole company moving in the same direction by getting the various functions to work together. The second role, though, is the most important: the CEO sets the direction in the first place. The direction a company is moving is not arbitrary—it must be thought out, taking into consideration the strengths of the company, the core goals of the leaders, and the movement of the markets. In others words, the vision and the strategy for the company are the CEO's responsibility.

Recently, in a talk I was giving, I shared the various roles that companies have and I asked the group what their Company of One was missing. One lady quickly spoke up and said, "I do not have a vision or a strategy." She could speak for most of us! We all need a vision and a strategy. We need to have some goals that drive us. We need to be working at something we care about and are passionate about. That is what makes work enjoyable.

DRIVE

In Daniel Pink's book, *Drive*, he explains the way people today are *really* motivated. While he is talking about motivating employees in his book, it can tell us a lot about motivating ourselves. Having coached hundreds of people directly and thousands indirectly, I can assure you this is what almost everyone wants.

First, we want autonomy. We all want the ability to control our own destinies. We all want the ability to see what needs to be done and to do it. In short, we hate micromanagers. Instead we want leaders who will cast a vision, inspire us to follow them, then get out of our way to let us work our magic.

Second, we want to become experts in what we do. We want the ability to continually learn so our Company of One will have a clear brand: what we uniquely do and what we are very skilled at doing. Whether we are a software developer, a surgeon, or a greeter, we want to be the best and be *known* for being the best!

Third, we want to be part of something that is meaningful. Nothing is more defeating to the human spirit than to be doing something we believe has no true purpose or meaning. We all want to make a difference and we all want to leave a legacy.

OF RACEHORSES AND MEN

But beyond the motivation factor, is really helps if we are doing the right thing—the things we are uniquely created to do. Rick Warren says in his audiocassette, *Growing Spiritually at Work,* that over 60% of Americans work in the wrong career field. I do not know where he gets his numbers, but my own experience tells me that this really is how most people feel about their work. And if this is true, it spells 'trouble.'

> *That is how many of us lead our lives–like racehorses giving pony rides!*

Ever deal with a spirited racehorse? They are full of tension and quick to spook. They have been bred for action, to play in the race, and make something happen. They cannot wait for the gate to open so they can burst forward. Now can you imagine all that energy tied up giving pony rides to kids? The horse would be a bundle of nerves, and since it is placed in the wrong job, it would be dangerous. Yet, that is how many of us lead our lives—like racehorses giving pony rides!

FUTURE PLANS - CORE/CALLING/CAREER/JOB

So, how do you get out of this trap, find out what you really want to do, and start making a move to do it? In other words, how do you start being a real CEO to your Company of One?

CORE

First, you need to determine your CORE. Over the course of your life, your jobs will change and your careers may change. Even the things you are called to do (your 'calling') may change. You may be a medical doctor today and become a farmer later. You may be a software developer who becomes a veterinarian (I know one of these).

A person's CORE will rarely change (though mine did when I accepted Christ). Your CORE is made up of those things you believe and hold true—those things that guide everything you do. Like the U.S. Constitution, which guides all governmental activity, your CORE is the cornerstone of all your personal and professional decisions. Like the Constitution, if we forget to focus on it, we will drift away from it.

For most people, their CORE is their religious beliefs. It is bigger than they are; it is immortal. Yet, for many people, their CORE beliefs get pushed aside when they make practical decisions. Years later they often find that they have drifted away and become something they never wanted to become. A job can lead you to compromise the truth and your integrity in the name of 'getting along' or 'being a team player.' If you look up and do not like the people you are working with because you do not like their ethics, then you had better look in the mirror, and hard.

So, now you need to find your CORE. Get back to what really matters. Get to the truth. In fact, write it down *now*—and perhaps take a moment to honestly evaluate if you are currently living your core.

My CORE is Jesus Christ. You do not have to agree with that, but I consider the Bible as truth. I do not have to be a preacher to live out my CORE, but I do have to do all things to the glory of God, including writing this book. I also find that it is critical to live out my faith on a daily basis.

What if you do not know what your CORE is? Or, what if your CORE is weak, or you are not sure that it is based in truth? I could not call Christ my CORE unless I had challenged it to be sure it was true. Maybe it is just me, but I need to *know* what I believe. I have wrestled with my faith in Christ, and I truly believe it is truth. You need to know yours is true, or you will be building on a weak foundation. If you have no CORE, or are not sure if you believe your CORE to be true, I suggest your career is not your biggest issue.

If you look up and do not like the people you are working with because you do not like their ethics, then you had better look in the mirror, and hard.

CALLING

Your calling is what you are called to do. You can take this in a biblical sense or in a DNA sense; it doesn't matter to me. But clearly, some people are wired to do particular activities and not others. Calling might also be labeled your passion. What are you passionate about? What drives you?

How would you answer the following questions?

- What did I want to do when I was a kid?
- What kinds of books do I read for fun?
- What do I love doing now?
- What do I wake up thinking about?
- What do I go to sleep thinking about?
- What do others ask me to help them do?

Maybe a better question is asked by Ann Rea (you'll meet her in a minute), "What can I *not* not do?"

Think about that for a minute. What can you *not* not do?

Here is how to figure it out for yourself. Write down the answers to the questions above. Do it now. Forget about laboring over each question, just write down what comes to mind. Take as much or as little time as you like, then put the answers away and do the same thing tomorrow. Do this each day for several days. Your mind will be racing all day long on this subject!

I used to tell people to do this differently. I told them to get in a comfortable place and relax. Then get a clean pad of paper and a pen and spend an hour working on this. The problem is, when I would meet with them weeks later, they would not have started to answer these questions because they had not felt they had the time. So just do it now and do *something*!

CAUTION: Most people will *not* write down things because just as it comes into their mind they will say to themselves, "I cannot do that" or "you cannot make a living doing that", etc. *Don't do this!* This is a brainstorming exercise. There are no wrong or 'bad' answers, so write it all down. You do not have to share this with anyone. Do not challenge your answers (you are not writing a contract; you're just recording thoughts). Do not let your own thoughts frighten you! Write them down. You never know when a crazy thought might lead you to something exciting.

These exercises are not magic. They are intended to make you *think*. The point now is to spend some time in the next few days considering what you are really after. If you have passion, put it down in writing now. Then you can develop a plan to turn this passion into your livelihood. Many people have done it and done it well.

Consider the story of Ann Rea. She paints for a living. We all know what that means: starving artist. That is very true for many artists—they starve. So if you were to write down, "I would love to do art," your first inclination may be to discount this idea as a great way to starve yourself and your family. In your head you would hear those voices saying, "you can't make a living doing that." Yet, Ann does—and a great living at that.

Ann found a way to make painting connect with the right customers and has built a thriving business. Check out her story on annrea.com. For more stories like Ann's, check out Jonathan Field's book, *Career Renegade*. You have to get past the desire to shoot down all your ideas which are based on conventional wisdom.

Read the *Reality Check* below—you need to understand that there is a business side to all of this. You have to figure out how to add value to others by doing what you love, but the first key is to find out what you love to do or would love doing by developing a list of your personal "assets." You can decide later if you want to turn this passion of yours into profit.

REALITY CHECK

Who would pay me to do what I love?

I know what you are thinking: who would pay me for doing what I love? Oprah Winfrey loves talking to people; who would ever pay for that? Look at the Food Network and the interviews with people who love to cook; who would pay for that? Think about all those professional sports figures playing games for a living; who would pay for that? Think about authors writing for a living; who would ever pay for that?

I was speaking to a group on this very subject and a man in the audience wanted to point out just how wrong I really was. He said, "I like Dallas Cowboy football. I bet you can't figure out how to make money off of *that!*" We all laughed; he was even wearing a Dallas Cowboys sweatshirt at the time.

I asked him, forgetting the players and the coaches, does anyone else make money off Dallas Cowboy football? The group chimed in to suggest as many as ten ideas for him including things like becoming a vendor at the games, selling Cowboy merchandise, etc. We did not really work too hard at it, but it's clear that a lot of people make money from the sport and the team.

He had a puzzled look and said, "well sure, but I'm a software developer." Assuming software was his passion, I asked if he thought the Cowboys had any software needs? Did they have an office and things to manage to make games, players, coaches, events, PR events, etc., all work together? The Cowboys are not just a team, they are an organization, and a lot of work must happen for us all to watch the team play on Sunday.

He got the point and, months later, he was planning hard to merge what he loved with his need to make a living. I do not know where he stands on it today, but at least he knows he has a choice now.

CAREER VS. JOB

OK, have you been thinking about these questions? Have you defined some things you love doing? This step is often a major struggle for people since we are rarely asked what we want. So the temptation is to keep on thinking. We tend to think we need to set aside hours, days, entire vacations just to get to the root of who we are.

If you can do that, great. Do it as soon as possible. But let's be practical. My experience tells me that people get caught in this struggle trying to "find themselves" for *years*. Fortunately some finally do, but many just continue to float around in a sea of indecision. So, instead, let's take action with what you have. After all, you are free to change direction as needed. Trust me, once you start moving in a direction toward what you love doing, you will find it is much easier to change course later if needed.

First, let's define some terms. Your career is how you make money from your calling, but, it is *not* a job. For instance, if I love working outside and keeping yards looking wonderful, I might find a career in yard work or landscaping. I did not say a *job*, but a *career*.

The job is how I am making money *today* from the career. So in my landscaping career, I might have a job with A&B Landscapes today. Or if I have gone into business for myself, I might have a job working for Mr. Smith today. In fact, if I am in business for myself I will likely have multiple jobs per day! I may lose one job, but that does not mean I am changing careers.

Dan Miller told me that his coaching has revealed that people do this backwards. They take a job, and after a while it defines them. It is not about what they love, it is just a job. Then when something happens to that job, they question their career and their calling. He has spent years coaching people caught in this crisis. The reason there is a crisis is because they did it all backwards.

Is your current "career" one that came from actually *planning* to do what you loved? Or, are you like I was: taking the job that was offered and then moving on to the next offer? Suddenly I was defined as a telecommunication expert, but the fact is, I couldn't really care less about that industry.

OK, enough background. Let's get to work. This is simple. Take the list of things you love to do (you *have* written it down, right?) and start writing down ways you can make money doing those things. Do not stop writing until you have at least 20 ideas. If you can only think of one (or none) now, come back to it later. Keep adding to the list over time. Again, once you start thinking about this, your mind will be in overdrive all day. Your antenna will help you see and hear things that look like opportunities.

CAUTON: Another caution is in order. Think about how you can get paid doing what you love, not how you can get a job. Forget about jobs and job titles and companies; who cares? You are brainstorming things that people will pay you to do. Again, *do not question yourself—just* write down your ideas, even if they sound stupid.

A lot of money has been made on "stupid" things. My friend Patrick Cash made over $100,000 from selling building plans for a cat scratching post. Simple? Perhaps. Stupid? If you say so. Patrick will gladly accept either definition. He made six figures on that 'stupid' idea. So, go ahead and be stupid.

The trouble with the corporate world is that it has caused many of us to kill our creativity. Patrick, instead of being simple and stupid, was filling a need. He delivered to people a solution to the very problem he himself had encountered—overpriced cat trees.

PURE MAGIC

OK, now you have a lot of ideas on paper. This next step is nothing short of pure genius. It is so powerful it will change your world, yet it is very simple.

Look over your lists and determine who is already doing those things. Who is doing what you love to do for a living? You may know them, or you may not. You may not come up with a single name. This task is about finding out who is living *your* dream. If you have to start searching the Internet to find them, that's OK. I know they are out there.

Next, contact those people and ask for a reverse interview (this will be detailed in the next chapter). The more successful these people are, the better. The people who can teach you how to get to where you want to be are the people who are already there. In the reverse interview, doors will fly open and opportunity will fly in.

The result of this meeting will help you develop the rest of your path. There are always more steps to take, but do not hesitate to start this process. There is nothing worse than getting caught up in a dream because of what you thought it would be like, only to have it dashed when you get a dose of reality. Sometimes what you thought would be a dream can turn out to be a nightmare. But every meeting and interview (even if done through email) will lead you into a new area. *To see a detailed example of this exercise, see Joe's story in the Appendix.*

BECOME PASSIONATE

OK, I hear many of you now: you are saying, "But I do not have a passion." In my seminars and training, I have worked with many people from high school students to CEOs. I ask them a question I will ask you now.

What do you want?

Simply question, right? Apparently not. Sure, I have a few people who immediately smile and tell me what they are passionate about doing. Often there is a central mission in their mind: people would benefit from what they want to do. But many people look perplexed. Here are some of the answers I received:

"No one has ever asked me that, and now that you have, I am at a loss."

"I have worked on this question for the last year since taking the course. I still do not have an answer."

"I want to serve people, but have no idea how."

"You asked me this question so often I thought you were crazy. I just wanted you to stop asking. But then I realized there is strategic focus in this—and I did not want to stop to think strategically about my life."

"This was the hardest assignment I ever had. I have never worked so hard on anything."

"BTW, this was the hardest thing to nail down as far as ideas are concerned! I have rewritten this so many times that I have to wear a wig and hat to keep my hair from sticking straight up in the air."

Clearly, for most of us, this is not an easy question. I am not sure why, but I partially understand since I can relate to each of the quotes above.

In every book on success you ever read, this question is asked in one form or another. I have struggled with it personally. It could be a case of attention deficit disorder or the inability to commit—I'm not really sure. Yet, one comment I got in the past seven years really hit home. It is from Rusty Hyde of Hyde Engineering:

> *"I find the struggle is that everyone is looking for their passion—that one thing that will finally light their fire and forge them ahead. But perhaps the key is not the search for passion, but to learn to become passionate."*

What a thought! A similar sentiment was written many years ago by a man named Paul:

> *"Not that I am speaking of being in need, for I have learned in whatever situation I am to be content. I know how to be brought low, and I know how to abound. In any and every circumstance, I have learned the secret of facing plenty and hunger, abundance and need. I can do all things through him who strengthens me."* Philippians 4:11-13

So, if you are like many of these people and cannot find their passion, perhaps you are looking for a *thing* when, in fact, you need an *action* around which to develop passion. You may need to *be a part* of something. In case you are thinking this is a cop-out and no one destined to be a leader would ever do this, think again.

In years of working with venture capital and startup companies, I have noticed a trend. Companies grow, and their founders have a great passion for the company and their product. Eventually the company is sold, money is made, and the technologies become part of a corporate machine. The company founders are often left looking around for something new. Over and over I see it—they are then looking for another good idea or another good team to either join or lead. They may no longer have the key idea or the passion about a *thing*, now they have a passion for the game.

Drew Deaton, one of these entrepreneurs, told me about a year ago, *"I am looking for a team to lead so we can build something together."*

Recently, Drew called to tell me that he had found his new passion: a start-up company called Vipaar, LLC. Drew has a new team with a new technology. He did not invent anything, but he is now their biggest evangelist. Watch this company—my bet is it will do well!

So, if you find yourself struggling to find something you are passionate about, you might instead be one of those people who is passionate about an action. In fact, many people are in this position. Think about these alternatives:

- I want to continually create.
- I want to be part of something that benefits the customer.
- I want to help my customers.
- I want to build something great.
- I want to be a key member of a team.
- I want to manage a process or a company.
- I love to communicate ideas to others.

Anything here strike you? Can you make your own list? Think about Michael Jordan again—he loves a *game*. Drew has a passion for finding healthcare solutions using technology and taking them to the market to change lives, even save lives. A lot of technology people are looking for an exciting company with a technology opportunity that makes a difference in the real world.

Beginning engineering students all want to make money. Engineering is known as a fast track to getting paid well. But if you talk to these students for any length of time, you will realize they also want to be part of something, to have an impact on the world. They want to save lives, save the earth, be part of the next space program, etc. They are passionate about the action. They are not ready to lead the team (most of them), but they want to be a part of it. The point is that I have found a lot of people fit this description—they're struggling to find passion within themselves.

People often tell me that they just want out or "I want out of corporate America." As they searched for something to be passionate about, one of these people recently said something profound:

"I do not want out, I want leadership. I want to find someone with a vision and a passion that has a team put together to make something happen—and I want to join that team."

Does this describe *you?*

DEVELOP YOUR COMPANY OF ONE

1. Has there ever been anything you wanted or dreamed of doing? (Even as a child) What is it?

2. What are the last five books you read?

3. Think of your job and company. Can you become passionate about anything there?

4. What is the mission or vision statement of your current employer? Does this mission/vision fit you?

5. If you have not already done it, do the CORE/ CALLING/ CAREER exercise.

6. Interview those who are living *your* dream!

11

NETWORKING FOR

INTROVERTS

"Question: How many introverts does it take to have a meeting?

Answer: It only takes two, but they both need to have a computer and an Internet connection." [1]

Do you remember when you were trying to land your first job? Remember the advice you got about writing a resume? Maybe you even took a class about writing a resume. When I was in engineering school, counselors would speak to us about developing a "well-crafted resume." Then they told us that most "jobs" did not come from ads or resumes, but instead from networking. So, we were told to network.

I was confused. They told us that what works is networking, not sending resumes, yet they spent their time teaching us to write resumes. They never *correctly* taught this introverted engineer or my classmates how to *network*.

As I have held and changed jobs over time, I have been troubled by this "education" I received. In fact, I have read articles and books that continue to state this conventional wisdom: *networking works*. The problem is that I was taught to write a resume but I was never really taught how to network. What little advice they did give me about networking seemed to reap limited success. Here is some of that common advice and what I found when I tried it:

Advice: Go to professional meetings to meet people.

Result: Ended up standing around knowing few people or meeting people in the same situation I was in. I never connected in any meaningful way to the people who could help me.

Advice: Tell everyone you know that you are looking for a job.

Result: Limited success. I did get to meet some people who were hiring managers, but it seemed my own network was not enough to get me in the doors I needed to get into.

Advice: Make use of college career fairs and career counselors.

Result: Again, limited success. I was limited to those companies looking for people like me, but *I* was looking for something *else*. The problem was that I did not really know what I was looking for—I just knew it was something else. I remember thinking at the end of one of these job fairs, "Is this all there is? I went into engineering to do something really powerful and have an impact on the world! All these jobs sound boring!"

But networking is about more than just finding a job. After many years of "playing the networking game", conducting job searches, and connecting to people in networking events, I have made some observations:

- People with a network have more opportunities. I cannot state this strongly enough! People who know people and have a network have many more opportunities.

- The world is *full* of opportunities! New jobs, new customers, new people to serve, new ways to make money. So many opportunities and so little time! Nothing seems to change this fact. Nothing—not even politics, the economy, the weather—nothing. Opportunity seems to abound everywhere and always.

- People work with people, not with resumes, business plans, or anything else on paper. All of our education tells us that well-documented plans and reports are critical to success. But nobody reads them! The only purpose of these documents is to help you get your head straight so you can communicate effectively when you are in your network. Introverts who are hunting for a job want to use their resume as their face and personality. But it doesn't work; it is a lifeless piece of paper.

- When it comes to the job search, resumes are an after-thought for many companies. My last few "jobs" did not really require a resume. In fact, more than once it came up that the resume was needed from me *after* the decision was made to hire me. One company told me to forward my resume to HR since they needed one on file.

- Even introverts can be power networkers. Yes, even introverts! In fact, some of the best networkers I know are self-proclaimed introverts.

- Networking is a skill most people do *not* have. Perhaps this is why I was never taught how to network—the teachers did not know how to do it themselves.

-

CONFESSION

Let me confess right up front: I hate going to networking events! I dread going to almost all of them, even when I know I will be among friends.

The night before an event, I almost always tell Lea that I am going to skip out on this one. She looks me in the eye and says, "You say that every time. Then you go and find a whole new business to start, a new partnership, or a new opportunity that excites you. Just *go*."

She is so right! I cannot tell you the number of times I have been at a meeting where a new company begins to form right before my eyes! I used to jump on every one of them, not wanting to miss out on the new endeavor. But now I have learned that opportunities are everywhere, and I am not just looking for *anything*, but for the *right* thing.

COMPANY OFFICERS KNOW YOU NEED TO NETWORK

Having worked with corporate officers from companies small to large, I see the other side of networking. These officers eat and breathe networking. They are planning for success. They know how to network and consider it critical to success. They need to interact with their customers and clients and they know they will uncover opportunities simply by networking. New opportunities rarely come from sitting at your desk!

The same is true for your Company of One! So you, too, should consider networking a critical activity. Most corporate employees have what Tim Taylor, a friend of mine and author of *Launch Fever,* calls "cubicle insanity." Tim says, for most people, their entire network is comprised of the people who come into their cube or the conference room down the hall. When things go bad in the company, none of the people in this limited network can help. None of these people will present a new opportunity beyond a promotion within the current company.

Exercise: List the people in your network.

- Who do you go to lunch with?
- Who can you call on if you are looking for a new job or opportunity?
- What group do you hang out with which presents new opportunities to you on a regular basis?

CEO AND CMO NETWORKING

Networking was a key ingredient in the CMO role, but we have delayed looking at it in detail until after we covered the CEO role. The reason is that networking is not only marketing, it is strategic. We should not go to networking events or meetings where the connections we make end up leading us in the wrong direction!

For instance, the CEO and CMO of a company that makes automobiles (let's say Ford) will get little strategic value from attending a conference geared toward marketing kitchen appliances. The event will be a huge waste of time for a Ford executive.

Executives need to be strategic with their time and networking. Who do they need to be meeting? Who are the key players that will help them get from where they are to where they want to go? Those are the people they need to be around.

So this is why I have waited to cover this subject. Who you meet needs to be about both marketing *and* strategy! Since we are looking at Company of One Networking, we know time is limited, so we need to make it count. Therefore, the networking skills provided here focus on marketing what you have in a way that will help get you where you want to go. In other words, your CEO and your CMO work together on this one.

REALITY CHECK

Brian Rabon is a self-proclaimed introvert. He was a client of mine through the IEM graduate program. He expressed a great interest in becoming more networked and getting to know the right people. Brian knew his job well, and he believed me when I said the world was filled with opportunity, but he did not know where to look. So I started showing him what I knew. I introduced him to people and got him placed in a few volunteer positions where I knew he could add value.

Within a year, I was getting calls from people who reported that Brian was a superstar who really delivered the goods. It really hit me when I went to a networking event where *I* normally knew everyone and found *Brian* introducing *me* to people!

When I tell people this they just say, "Brian, an introvert? You're nuts; he's *everywhere!*"

NETWORKING 101

OK, let's get down to it!

First, go back and look at the question, "What do I want?" What do you want to do? Networking means interacting with people, but *intentional* networking means interacting with the *right* people. Who can contribute to meeting your goals? If you are a software developer who really wants to become a homebuilder, what value is it to hang out with other software developers? By chance, one of them might be a valuable connection to home building, but we have chosen not to live by chance anymore!

Second, who is doing it now? Who is living your dream? Who is years ahead of you? If you want to be a state senator, to whom would you go for advice? Most people would ask their friends and co-workers, who would likely be full of free, but worthless, advice. Why not go to someone who is established? Find the most well-known and most well-established state senators you can find. They should be easy to find. No matter what it is you want to do, you can be sure that someone has been there before.

Third, contact them and get advice. This step is where the intimidation factor really kicks in! I find we are often intimidated by people who seem to have reached success. Even if these people are not celebrities or officers of large companies, I find that my clients, more often than not, dread this step of making contact and asking for advice. So here are some suggestions:

1. **Do you know someone** who can introduce you to the person you want to talk to? If so, boldly ask for an introduction, then ask for a meeting. If this person is living your dream, you need to talk to them. But even better is to call your network and ask for an introduction. You might ask them both to lunch, or at the very least request an introductory email. I personally prefer to contact the person I want to talk to via email and say something like:

   "Joe Smith (your common connection) suggested I contact you. I want to get into the home building business and would like to chat with you about how you got started and any advice you have for someone who is new to the business."

   I would copy Joe Smith on the message. For me, this type of email gets straight to the point and gets the fastest result.

2. **Use tools such as LinkedIn and other social media**. Make contacts in this public forum. Take some time to get to know them and what makes them tick, but not *too* much time. Ask for a meeting ASAP! I have found social media to be a powerful connecting tool. Everyone is equal on social media.

   The wonderful thing about such tools is that when you connect to others, they will one day be asking *you* for help. Recently David Riklan, owner of Self Growth.com (the largest website on the topic of self improvement on the web) contacted me via LinkedIn and asked me for a connection to Dan Miller, author of *No More Dreaded Mondays*. In my view, they did not need me to connect them. But David has built his company by making his network work for him, and even after 10 years and huge growth, he is still making it work today. I gladly made the connection.

3. **Cold call**. If you do not have a contact, do not be afraid of cold calling! I am often amazed with the results people discover from boldly calling someone they do not know and asking for help and advice. I have done this myself on many occasions.

While looking at a book on Amazon one day, I read a review written by a guy named Henry Devries and thought, "I need to talk to this guy." Not the author of the book, but Henry! Something he said in the review made me realize that he was doing exactly what I was trying to do, so I looked him up and sent an email:

Henry,

I found your name when you reviewed the book, Money Talks: How to Make a Million as a Speaker, *on Amazon. I was intrigued since you live a duplicate life. I, too, find myself in this situation with a company that sells products and an academic appointment. However lately I am finding a strong demand in the market for what I teach: entrepreneurship. My focus is helping people in corporate America find alternatives. I am looking at how to spin this out, and it appears you have done something similar. Would love to talk to you and learn how you balance this, and most important how you got it moving.*

If we could chat over the phone (I am in Alabama) that would be perfect. I know this time can be busy, so just let me know if you are willing to give me a number. Or call me if you like at 205-555-1212.

Thanks,
Dale

The next day, I got an email from Henry and we lined up a time to talk over the phone (he is on the other side of the country, so lunch was not practical). I spent the whole of 15 minutes on the phone with Henry and got invaluable advice! I found out that he was very skilled in helping people market professionally.

Avoid the temptation to talk to the mildly successful. I know what you may be thinking: "a very successful person will not want to talk to me. They will not have time for me." You may be right. They may be hard to get to. But, I have found that the more successful a person is, the more willing they are to provide advice to eager newbies. Many highly successful people have told me they feel obligated to give back and help others along.

Fourth, have an agenda. When you do get to talk to the person who is living your dream, be ready to do a few things:

- Let them talk! The temptation may be to talk about yourself. Some think, "Now that I am with this successful person, I can sell myself into their organization." Forget it. If you do this, you have forgotten your objective. What you want is to hear *their* story.

> People love to talk about themselves and they generally like people who encourage them to talk about themselves.

- Ask questions. Start with something like, "I have a desire to become a (*insert your desire here*) and I wanted to know how to get there. Can you tell me how you got started?" This is a powerful question. Tim Taylor often uses this approach out of his natural curiosity. Tim is amazing to watch. He asks questions naturally. He just wants to know people's stories. By asking this question, he does not get answers like how the company did last year or a standard marketing pitch. Instead, he learns about the passion, education, work history, etc. that brought these people to where they are today. It is a personal question. You are not asking about what a state senator does, but asking *how they got there*. And yes, Tim has a *huge* network of people who consider him a friend.

- Ask two other key questions: "What do you *love* about what you do?" and "What do you *hate* about what you do?"

The point of these questions is to make things personal and get these people to talk about themselves. A key point in Dale Carnegie's famous book, *How to Win Friends and Influence People,* is that people love to talk about themselves and they generally like people who encourage them to talk about themselves. (Think about your friends and people you really like to be around. Do they ask questions because they want to hear about you?)

Fifth, follow up. This is *critical*! Immediately follow up with a thank-you email, card, or something else. It may seem silly and meaningless to you, but it isn't to them. If you have been on the other side of the networking game, you understand. When I am approached with one of these questions about what I love to do or when I get a follow-up email, I understand what they are doing, but I still feel a special connection with these people.

Some people *know* what to do, and others actually *do* it. I have great respect for those who take the time to do it. Even if all I do is delete their thank-you email, their action was still noticed and appreciated.

Another way to follow up is to add value to them. Did you just learn of something they would appreciate knowing about? Do you know someone they would like to know? Immediately send this information to them while thanking them for their time. The point of the follow-up is to keep the contacts alive.

REPEAT

I recommend you do this at least ten times. I understand that this may be way out of your comfort zone—if so, great! Take the challenge and grow. Some of the results you should expect include:

- The names, email addresses, and phone numbers of people doing what you would like to do. You just increased your network.
- These people will like you. How do I know? Simple: you asked them to talk about themselves.
- Knowledge. Yes, now instead of *thinking* you want to do something, you now know something about it. You might have decided you do not like the idea of being a state senator anymore—if so, consider this a big success. Nothing is worse than dreaming about something you end up not wanting anyway. Now you know.

It is likely that you might also get the following:

- Exponential growth of your network. The likelihood is that a single contact will introduce you to three or more other people. Once someone likes you, they will be quick to introduce you to others in their organization. I have had a cold call result in meeting ten people in a single outing. (But no, these people do not count as the repeat since all of these people have a common relationship. You will not get the full story with just one set of connections.) I have people come to me weekly asking for advice on one thing or another, and they always walk away with an introductory email to a few other people who I feel will benefit them.

- A job. Yes, I said a job. I know, you're not asking for one. (You should *never* ask for a job during this meeting—the purpose of the meeting is to *learn*.) But, the fact is that most companies are looking for good people. The best person is one they like and one who is interested in the job and career path. By asking the questions you have asked, you will fit these objectives and may get offered a job. Perhaps this is hard to believe, but it happens *often*. If you do get an offer, politely tell them you are just trying to learn right now and are not ready to make a move. This is important to keep your integrity. If you decide you like what they had to offer, you can call back later and tell them you are looking for a position now. They will remember you; they are part of your network.

REALITY CHECK

Delayed Reaction

Frank Flow, a client of mine, was doing reverse interviews (the process we just described) with sales organizations just as an exercise to meet people. Frank sold industrial equipment, and he wanted to learn a bit about how sales people approached other markets. One of the people he interviewed was a salesperson in a large financial firm. Frank conducted the interviews, learned a lot, and then went about his business. Months later, the financial company called him. They were very impressed by his approach to learn more and they offered him a job. He took it!

That is great news, but I just got off the phone with Frank, and he added a little more perspective to what happened. He said that in a typical interview you are being sized up to see if you fit in 'the box'—to see if you match the job they need to fill. But, in the reverse interview, there is no box. Instead they get to know you first.

Frank explained that the job he was offered was not normally advertised; it was a situation where they needed to know the right person to reach out to and hire. They were looking for a specific type of individual, and one of the leaders remembered Frank as matching what they needed. As Frank said, "I got the position I wanted to get instead of the position they typically hired for."

Now it's your turn. Try it. Force yourself if you have to. *Just do it.*

NETWORKING 102

A second powerful and often overlooked method to increase your network is through professional organizations. I know, this is the advice you were given in college, but here is the rest of the story.

First, like always, decide what you want. There are millions of organizations and associations to choose from. You need to know where your efforts should be placed. Again, why go to a software developer meeting when you want to build homes? Find an organization where like-minded people gather instead.

Second, use your Networking 101 contacts. You know who you want to meet: the person who is actually doing what you want to do. They are already part of these organizations. Rather than showing up blind and not knowing anyone, show up with one of the movers and shakers of the organization. Then you immediately get introduced and connected at the highest level. Remember to not talk about yourself too much—let other people talk. You should become skilled at asking questions.

Third, take action. Every volunteer organization, no matter the size, struggles from having a lot of takers and very few givers. The decision makers in a thousand-member organization can likely fit around a small conference table. They are the ones who give their time and actually *do* something. So your trick is to find out where they really need help and do it. The result is that you will not be a nameless figure, instead everyone will know you and *know* that you get things done.

Fourth, do it. People are *always* watching and judging. They will assume the character you display within the organization is your character, and they are right. Remember, this is a part of your brand! If you show up and do what you promised, they will think highly of you.

When you do make a commitment, *make it happen*. If something prevents you from keeping your promise, find a way to make it right. Do not ignore failures. Be frank and up-front about them and seek to correct the poor impression you made. Few people acknowledge when they have failed. An honest apology and an attempt to make things right could turn things around and leave a wonderful impression.

NETWORKING 103

People often make great contacts only to later lose them. The job gets busy, years pass, and suddenly you look around and have another case of cubicle insanity. Your great new job or career has turned sour and things are not as pretty as they once were. You have failed to keep up your contacts and grow them.

Remember, company owners know the value of networking. Also remember, you are indeed a Company of One, so you must continue to network—*always*—even if you are happy in your current job. Here are a few ideas to help you continually add contacts to your network:

- **Take a lunch.** Invite key people on your contact list to lunch. It's a great way to stay connected. People, even busy people, go to lunch—especially if you pay, but that is not critical. Get out of the trap of lunching with the same people every day.

- **Use email wisely.** Touch base with your contacts often. As your list grows, you will have to focus on key contacts only, but that is a good problem to have. Ask questions and provide information they may be interested in knowing. Now that you know them and what they like, you can be on the lookout for opportunities to give back to them.

- **Ask them to speak.** The number-one problem with most professional organizations is that they have a difficult time lining up interesting speakers for their meetings. These organizations tend to invite the same small group of speakers over and over. You can ask your contacts to speak at these meetings. No matter what their title or how busy they are, people always feel honored when asked to speak. Even if they have to send one of their employees instead, you are still the hero for the organization, and you have now met someone new. (This is also a great way to make new contacts. Speakers usually only remember the person who invited them to speak.)

The point is to stay connected. Of course, this list is far from complete—these are just ideas to get you started. Make sure you use tools such as MS Outlook or LinkedIn to manage your contacts. Have their names, numbers, emails, and other relevant information in the system. Grow your list.

My contacts list is very important to me, and it grows and gets updated often. It is important because these are people I share things with. I am always looking out for ways to help my contacts. I share ideas and opportunities with them, and they do the same for me. Certainly, you will not be well connected to all of them in your list, but you will have *some* connection. As the list grows to hundreds (or thousands) of contacts, you will find some of them become rich and rewarding relationships on many levels.

NETWORKING 201

THE REVERSE INTERVIEW

CAUTION: This next networking tool is *powerful*! I tell people it is a guaranteed way to get a job, and I mean it. I have never seen anyone use this method who did not get a job offer!

OK, forget the networking basics. Now you want to start networking with a powerful purpose. You have grown to understand that you are indeed a Company of One and are looking for raw opportunity in places you may not have seen before.

We all know that most of the jobs in America are not listed in the paper, websites, or other help-wanted boards. (If you do not know this, read *What Color is Your Parachute?*) But here is a really scary, or exciting, thought, depending on how you look at it: you can create jobs that never existed!

REALITY CHECK

Challenge the idea

It was a few years after I had graduated, and I had little experience as a telecom engineer. I read the book, *What Color is Your Parachute?*, which claimed that people would offer you jobs when you did the reverse interview. The author, Richard Bolles, warned NOT to take the jobs, and for the same reasons I have already mentioned. But when I read his words about being offered a job without asking for one, I was sure Bolles was a nut-case. I thought he must be really cocky to think his method works so well that you did not even have to ask for a job to get an offer. I had to challenge him.

So, strictly out of my own desire to prove him wrong, I had to try it. I was careful to follow his steps: to make a call, ask the questions he suggested, then spend only 15 minutes with the person.

Even though I was an engineer, I had some desire to get into finance. I was interested in helping people with money. So I cold-called the owner of a financial services company. I did not know the guy; I just looked him up in the Yellow Pages, called him direct, and asked to speak to the owner. Again, I had no experience, just an interest. I asked for 15 minutes, which he gave me.

When we met, I expressed my interest and then listened, asking questions as they fit. Then I asked him, "What do you love about what you do?" and of course, "What do you hate about what you do?" When the 15 minutes was over, I was getting up and thanking him for his time as I walked to the door. He said, "We have not taken on new people in the last five years, and we do not have any positions open, but would you be interested in working with us?" I was floored! Walking out to my car I realized that Bolles' method worked! Then, as I started my car, I realized the rest of the story. I had just created a job. And, I was the only person being considered for the position!

In *Networking 101*, I talked about how you can interview a person who is doing what you want to do. I also warned you that you might get a job offer. But the odd thing is that there may not have been a job to offer! Many employers, especially officers, have the view that when they find good people, they hire them. Once the right people are hired, they can figure out where they belong in the organization. They do not hire positions, they hire people. And, by the way, this is the wisest way to hire people!

So when you are ready to really uncover some opportunities, try *Networking 201*. Set up a meeting with a current or new contact, and ask them these questions:

What are the biggest problems in your business?

What are the biggest problems in your industry?

What keeps you awake at night?

If you could do one thing to really improve your bottom line, what would it be?

What opportunities do you think your business should be going after?

These questions cut to the heart of the business. They are personal at some level, but beyond the "what do you love?" issues. These questions get at the heart of the "what will you pay for?" issues. Be aware, these questions might cause some surprise and may be difficult to answer. But if you get any answers (you likely will), you will have found very strategic issues to conquer. Now you have to ask: *Do any of these problems excite me? Can I solve them?*

If you *are* interested and you *can* solve those problems, you now have a possible new source of income. Go back to them to talk more about their issue. Never assume in one meeting that you really understand it all. Learn all you can, then come up with a solution and go present it. The rest (how much your solution costs) is negotiable.

REALITY CHECK

Many companies have started just this way. Gary York went to CEOs of hospitals trying to understand where he could start a new business using technology in healthcare. He had built one company in this area. He used his contacts to get in the doors of CEOs, then asked them what their problems were. He walked away with some common issues and problems. He solved one of them and partnered with one of the people he interviewed. The company he built is called Awarix, and in 2007, he sold it to McKesson Corporation. As you might guess, this is one of thousands of examples of networking which created opportunities.

SUGGESTIONS TO SUPERCHARGE YOUR CMO'S NETWORKING ABILITY

1. Do *Networking 101* with ten people. Take notes and remember to update your contacts.

2. Contact and interview four company officers. I recommend you start at the top. Ask them these questions:

   What are the biggest problems in your business?

   What are the biggest problems in your industry?

   What keeps you awake at night?

   If you could do one thing to really improve your bottom line, what would it be?

   What are the opportunities you think your business should be going after?

3. Invite people to lunch from other backgrounds and ask them the following questions. Who you invite does not matter. They can even be people you know, but try to get a balance between people you know well and those you don't. Be careful not to talk too much or get into a gripe session about your job. Ask:

   What business are you in?

   How did you get started in this work?

   What do you love about your job?

   What do you hate about your job?

   What is the biggest problem you have in your job?

APPENDIX - AN EXAMPLE OF

JOE'S CALLING

Here is an example of Joe's Calling and Career exercise. Joe is an example, loosely based on people I have consulted.

JOE'S BACKGROUND

Joe is a software developer with a *Fortune* 500 organization. The group he works for is responsible for testing software before deployment to the customer base. Joe had been on the test team, but began to develop software tools to assist his testing team—his tool development then became his full-time job. He had developed software, which allowed the group to develop and track test plans and track the amount of time used to test each product, as well as to document the bugs found.

His director noticed Joe's expertise in adding value to the team. When the director was under the gun to show how the whole test team added value to the company, Joe was asked if his tools could help quantify results. Joe helped the director develop a model of value based on the number of software bugs found per product and industry studies of the cost of bugs being released to the public. Using this information, Joe and the director developed a model to show the real monetary value the team added in terms of how much the group saved the company and subtracted the costs of the team, which were mainly salaries. Joe determined that his team added $13 million per year to the organization in addition to intangible customer satisfaction benefits.

Joe loves his work, but he is constantly getting new direct managers—some are great leaders; others are micromanagers. While Joe loves his work, the bureaucracy and frustrations of the *Fortune* 500 is starting to 'get' to him. So Joe starts to examine his Company of One. Let's look at some things he discovered while completing the Calling and Career exercise.

Here is Joe's list of what he loves to do and how he loves to work. Notice that this is a loose brainstorming list:

- o Software development, but cannot do this all day long; not focused enough; I'm too ADD for that and can only code for about two hours.
- o Guitar for fun.
- o I like a flexible work schedule; I hate 8 to 5.
- o Helping others via applications; it's fun to assist others.
- o I really enjoyed justifying the group's value through developing the models.
- o I like to travel on my own terms (not rushed).
- o I do not like being stuck in the office all day.
- o I like being able to meet people, even though I am an introvert, I enjoy interacting with others in small groups or one-on-one.
- o I like being around people who are positive and upbeat or bringing an upbeat attitude to the people.
- o I like helping people manage their money.
- o I always wanted to be a boss/CEO.
- o People ask me for technical help (fixing PCs, etc.) and I enjoy helping them.
- o I enjoy technology, but I'm not in love with it; do not read about the latest Windows release etc.; not into the geek model.
- o I enjoy thinking big picture instead of details.
- o I like project work—not the same thing every day.

Now with his list in hand, Joe begins to look at how he can make money from the things he enjoys. Notice this new list includes *ideas*, not solid plans:

- o Software consultant
- o PC repair tech
- o Field support for company with remote computer apps
- o Software developer for smaller company
- o Teach/coach software developers
- o Guitar teacher
- o Traveling instructor of software (such as a Microsoft trainer)
- o Consulting to help companies / teams develop a model of value added
- o Freelance software developer via elance.com or odesk.com (small projects fast)
- o Financial planner
- o Move up the current corporate ladder
- o Do training videos or books on software development
- o Write books and speak/teach people how to measure their value
- o Teach software developers and support people how to measure their value
- o My own company as a consultant or independent contractor
- o Write about money management blogs/books
- o Strategic planner (big picture stuff)
- o Strategic planner for software projects (software architect)
- o Support for software projects.

Notice that some of these ideas are fuzzy and some even overlap. One of the reasons for this is that Joe, while pretty smart, does not really know the details of what it means to be a consultant or independent software developer. Who would be his customers? What would be his niche? But that does not matter yet, because he is just exploring at this point.

Now Joe looks at this list. What really stands out? In which areas does he see overlap? He notices those in bold below are the ones that seem to show up a lot—they are related and seem to identify a particularly keen interest of his. This is why it is important to force yourself to keep putting ideas on paper: trends begin to appear even if you are unaware of them.

o   Software consultant
o   PC repair tech
o   Field support for company with remote computer apps
o   Software developer for smaller company
o   **Teach/coach software developers**
o   Guitar teacher
o   **Traveling instructor of software (such as a Microsoft trainer)**
o   **Consulting to help companies / teams develop a model of value added**
o   Freelance software developer via elance.com, odesk.com, gofreelance.com (small projects fast)
o   Financial planner
o   Moving up the corporate ladder
o   Do training videos or books of software development
o   **Write books and speak/teach people how to measure their value**
o   **Teach software developers and support people how to measure their value**
o   **My own company as a consultant or independent contractor**
o   Write about money management blogs/books
o   **Strategic planner (big picture stuff)**
o   Strategic planner for software projects (software architect)
o   Support for software projects.

Now Joe has some common threads to work with. He seems to be leaning toward some kind of consulting—helping people demonstrate how they add value to their organizations. He now needs to explore who is doing this type of work. Here is his list:

o   Consultants: specifically those in technology (perhaps those who help groups defend their roles? Who would that be?)

o   Authors of non-fiction books on subjects related to work and technology

o   Corporate trainers

o   Highly successful freelance consultants.

After talking to and interviewing several people, Joe learned a *lot* about how things really work. He interviewed consultants, trainers, authors, bloggers and noticed that they tend to be one and the same. But the key is to define your market and who you will serve, so Joe developed a plan.

JOE'S PLAN IN THE ROUGH

- Keep my day job, get better control, and add more value (cash cow). I can add more value and take more internal control—and I can put up with the garbage that goes with it for now.

- Get better positioned financially. Save more money in an emergency fund in case a downsizing hits me or I just cannot stand it anymore. Goal: one year's worth of expenses.

- I can begin *now* as a consultant to help people to measure their value. I can start by becoming an authority through speaking as a volunteer while I develop my model. I also can start a blog/newsletter on the subject, and help people that way. I can do this *and* add value to my current employer at the same time and be supported by them since it is directly related to my day job. Speaking and blogging will be supported as long as I do not give away confidential information. I will meet with my director to make sure he supports my desire to help others.

- Begin to offer my expertise in other parts of the company. Who can I offer to help? Can I get my director to support this? Can my director demonstrate that this effort is more value added to the company by his group?

- Try to land a single company contract or set up a training class to show people via webinar how to calculate their own value. Do this either outside of work time or with the agreement to do it during work hours by my employer. Begin developing a following and creating a list of people who come to my classes.

- Write a book on the subject and sell it to further define my authority.

- o Keep adding income via training and simple consulting gigs.

- o Slowly develop my consulting income until it can replace that of my day job.

Much of Joe's plan is undefined, but he does have a rough outline of how to develop expertise. The details do not matter much—his general vision is the key. The details will become more obvious the further he progresses through his plan. In the meantime, Joe wants to work with his current employer to create a win/win situation.

Joe's Overall Vision: to be a consultant who travels while providing training, and to sell books and other materials about how to measure value—and to make $250,000 per year doing this.

AFTERWORD

"Things may come to those who wait...but only the things left by those who hustle." Abraham Lincoln

A lot of ground has been covered here. If you have been doing the work, you have answered a lot of questions. But, if you are like me, you now have even more questions. But now it is time to do something else: *act!*

If you are a procrastinator who says, "I will do that part later", then find that part which struck you most and *act on it.* If you tend to doubt what you read, great—I love working with people who challenge my ideas! But first, you must act. Try out some of these things, then let me know how it worked out for you.

Either way, you cannot get anywhere simply by reading—not this book or any other. You will gain knowledge and perhaps perspective, and maybe at times be entertained, but action is key. So go hustle. Make something happen *today!* In fact, make something happen *every* day. That should be your plan: to take action daily toward your major life goal and toward becoming a better Company of One.

Let me know how it is going! I love to hear how people are taking control of their Company of One. Please contact me and let me know how your journey is going and what you have learned.

Email: dcallahan@uab.edu   Twitter: twitter.com/DaleCallahan

Blog: www.dalecallahan.com   Facebook: www.facebook.com/dalecallahan

LinkedIn:
www.linkedin.com/in/dalecallahan

And, of course, snail mail is still welcome!

Dale Callahan, HOEN 370, 1530 3rd Ave. South, Birmingham, AL 35294-4440

And remember to visit ResumesAreWorthless.com!

RECOMMENDED RESOURCES

For most of you, this book is about changing the way you *think*! But to continue the process you need to invest in learning, so you need to build a personal library.

SETTING THE GUIDELINES

Sometimes we need to make sure we have our head screwed on right before we take a leap into something. Often, we can find ourselves running from one thing to the next as a result of deciding what we do *not* like. I see this all too often with my clients—they can articulate very well what they hate, but are not very sure what is central and important. The books listed here focus on getting things right, strategically, in your life, business, and finances.

The 7 Habits of Highly Effective People, Stephen R. Covey

While we see Covey's book even in the corporate setting, it is really a book about leadership starting with yourself. Too many people dive into activities never having really examined their own priorities. They look back years later and wonder why they followed the crowd instead of doing what mattered most to them. Covey's book really helps focus on what is key. A bit of a hard read for many people since he comes off a bit academic, but the exercises are still valuable.

Business by The Book, Larry Burkett

In this classic, Larry Burkett uses biblical principles to demonstrate how they guide business. While you might flip through and think most of the principles are obvious, a closer read has Larry relating many stories about how the principles have worked in real life. An excellent read for those who have decided they want to focus on seeking the kingdom first.

The Total Money Makeover, Dave Ramsey

Dave Ramsey's advice is right on target. For most of us in the "want it now" culture we first need a bit of education—which comes in the form of a swift kick in the wallet. Dave offers this in steady doses. The principles in the book apply to running a business as well as running a household budget.

CHANGING YOUR THINKING

These books challenge the way you think—and if you have been raised in a government education system and/or have been living in the corporate world, you *really* need to change your thinking! In fact, your thinking is your Number One hurdle to creating positive change in your life!

Rich Dad Poor Dad, Robert T. Kiyosaki

While I would strongly argue against some later advice offered by Robert and his business partners, this one little classic really tells the truth. How the rich use money differently than the poor is key. I highly recommend this book. It's easy to read as well as entertaining.

No More Dreaded Mondays, Dan Miller

Many people I have suggested this book to have come back to me blown away by Dan's advice and outlook. If you are really stuck in the corporate grind and do not see hope, this book will help lift your spirits. You will start to see the possibilities. Dan hits home where most of us are: stuck in our thinking. His idea of "Fire yourself" is a solid plan for many of you. Again, an easy read with lots of inspirational stories.

Four-Hour Work Week, Timothy Ferris

The title says it all. Timothy really challenges our assumptions about the way we work. A lot of detail for your CRO to consider! Entertaining as well.

BREAKING AWAY FROM CORPORATE AMERICA

At one time in the not-so-recent past, the gold standard for success was the Harvard MBA—a degree and network which prepared you for the future on the fast track of corporate America. Yet today we are living in a time of the disappointed, or perhaps disgruntled, employee. For the reasons covered in this book, many of you are looking for an alternative. Over and over I hear the words, "I just want out of corporate America." These books should help pave your way.

Crush It!, Gary Vaynerchuk

Gary, of WineLibrary TV, is candid. He tells it like it is and suggests we learn to do the same. In other words, be authentic. If you are familiar with branding and social media tools, this book is very helpful and a fast, fun read. If you are not, you will still get value from the message.

Escape from Cubicle Nation, Pamela Slim

Pamela does a wonderful job walking you though much of the baggage you carry as you try to break out of corporate America. While Dan's *No More Dreaded Mondays* is wonderful on this front also, Pamela really does some hand-holding—walking you through the steps and quoting from many other authors and experts. A great book which will take you down a journey. It is not a casual read.

Book Yourself Solid, Michael Port

Michael Port is focused on developing a consulting or sales business in this book, but the principles work well with the Company of One. Michael does a great job helping you define your customers—something that, sadly, many mature businesses do not do very well. One of the biggest mistakes I see start-ups making is trying to cater to everyone—this is a recipe for disaster. Michael's book picks up where several others leave off on developing the right strategy to target your customers.

Good to Great, Jim Collins

I see this book mentioned on almost every successful entrepreneur's reading list. Some companies have made this required reading for their staffs. Collins starts out academic—examining company histories and comparing those that have made it to those who have not. Then, what created these differences is presented for us to use. It should be noted that some of the lessons may, in fact, be the result of Jim's wrong conclusion, but so far, many other company leaders agree with Jim's conclusions, so if you follow his lead, you are in great company.

The 21 Irrefutable Laws of Leadership, John Maxwell

John has the market on leadership books—I think he must release a new one each month. Most leaders would agree that he does a great job getting to the real lessons of leadership. John picks up where Steven Covey leaves off, going beyond personal exploration and into the relationships between leaders and the people who follow them. One thing I agree with 100% is his statement that "everything rises and falls on leadership" even in the smallest of companies. And something I have discovered on my own: those who think they are great leaders are usually wrong.

Career Renegade, Jonathan Fields

This is a great book to use to force yourself to think while you are doing the Career and Calling exercises. Jonathan uses plenty of examples of people who have figured out how to do what they love. Very inspiring and entertaining.

CLASSIC PRINCIPLES

The following books proclaim some timeless principles—no matter what the technology and no matter what the career path or industry. They lay the foundation for success—namely, how to influence people, how to network, and how to deliver results.

How to Win Friends and Influence People, Dale Carnegie

Dale nails people and how they think—yes, even you and me. His book can be summarized by saying, "if you want people to like you, get them to talk about themselves." But the book has much more to say to back this up and use it for building businesses and relationships. The only downside is that the book talks about business people and businesses as if we should be familiar with them, though many examples come from sixty years ago. Regardless, the stories are still relevant.

What Color Is Your Parachute?, Richard Nelson Bolles

Richard's books were the reason for my challenging the idea of the reverse interview. This book is a classic for job/career changers. It includes quite a bit of personal exploration about what you love to do and what kind of work you enjoy. It then has some great job hunting tactics that are out-of-the-box thinking. The book has a weird layout and structure, but it is still very useful.

The Go-Getter: A Story That Tells You How to be One, Peter B. Kyne

I got this one from a Dave Ramsey group I attended. A great book with a great story demonstrating what it really means to be a go-getter. This book lays out a clean picture of the person we *all* want to hire.

◊ ◊ ◊

I read all the time! I have tons of books on my shelf to read, and I am constantly being sent new ones. I will update my blog with the good stuff.

www.DaleCallahan.com

www.ResumesAreWorthless.com

MORE FROM DALE CALLAHAN

Dale uses his blog to share and communicate similar ideas about becoming a Company of One. Visit it and sign up for an email feed: www.dalecallahan.com. Also check out ResumesAreWorthless.com!

If you have the Entrepreneur bug, you will want Dale's course, *Discovering the Entrepreneur in You*. This course is in audio workbook form and was developed from an eight-week seminar on entrepreneurship. It includes all printed transcripts and worksheets needed and is available through Amazon.com, from his blog at www.dalecallahan.com, or from AskDrCallahan.com

The IEM program—an executive masters program in engineering management—is available from the University of Alabama at Birmingham. Alumni of the program regularly report this 20-month experience as life-changing. Dale acts as Director of the program and also teaches Company of One and Technology Entrepreneurship during the program. For details see www.uab.edu/iem.

Homeschooling parents will be interested in Dale's company AskDrCallahan, which prepares high school homeschoolers for college by delivering math courses and support/coaching for parents and their children. Courses include *Algebra*, *Geometry*, *Algebra II with Trig*, and *Calculus*—all taught at a university level. For details see www.AskDrCallahan.com.

REFERENCES

Chapter 1

1. Thinkexist.com, "Muhammad Ali quotes," thinkexist.com/quotation/it-s_just_a_job-grass_grows-birds_fly-waves_pound/215261.html (accessed May 11, 2010).
2. Brian Tracey, *Eat that Frog!* (San Francisco: Berrett-Koehler Publisher, 2007.)

Chapter 2

1. Seth Godin, *Linchpin.* (New York: Portfolio, 2010.)
2. The Conference Board, "U.S. Job Satisfaction at Lowest Level in Two Decades," www.conference-board.org/utilities/pressDetail.cfm?press_ID=3820 (accessed May 11, 2010.)
3. Gallup Poll as reported in June 2002 Entrepreneur Magazine. www.entrepreneur.com/magazine/entrepreneur/2002/june/51964.html (accessed May 11, 2010).
4. Scott Reaves, "Loving the Job Your Hate." December 1, 2005, www.forbes.com/carers/2005/11/30/career-work-employment-cx_sr_1201bizbasics.html (accessed May 11, 2010).

5. CNN Feb 3, 2005, edition.cnn.com/2005/BUSINESS/02/03/monday.pressure/index.html (accessed May 11, 2010.)

6. Dan Miller, *No More Dreaded Mondays*. (New York: Broadway books, 2008.)

7. CDC as reported on ProHealth. www.prohealth.com/me-cfs/blog/boardDetail.cfm?id=1191430 (accessed May 11, 2010).

8. Kim Kahn, "The Basics: How does your debt compare?," moneycentral.msn.com/content/savinganddebt/p70581.asp. (accessed May 11, 2010.)

9. Rabbi Daniel Lapin, *Thou Shall Prosper*. (Hoboken: John Wiley & Sons, 2002.)

Chapter 3

1. Earl Nightingale, *Lead the Field. (New York: Nightingale-Conant, 2002.)*

2. Steve Jobs, "You've got to find what you love," news.stanford.edu/news/2005/june15/jobs-061505.html (accessed May 18, 2010.)

3. Laurence Leamer, *Fantastic: The Life of Arnold Schwarzenegger* (New York: St. Martin's, 2005), 66.

4. Dan Miller, "Go Ahead — Make More Mistakes," 48daysblog.wordpress.com/2008/12/11/go-ahead-make-more-mistakes-2 (accessed August 9, 2010.)

5. Jack Canfield, *The Success Principles*. (New York: Harper Collins, 2005.)

Chapter 4

1. BrainyQuote, "Robert Orben Quotes," www.brainyquote.com/quotes/quotes/r/robertorbe103699.html (accessed August 5, 2010).

2. Alan Weiss, *Million Dollar Consulting*. (New York: McGraw Hill, 2009.)

Chapter 5

1. BrainyQuote, "Thomas J. Watson Quotes" www.brainyquote.com/quotes/quotes/t/thomasjwa125789.html (accessed August 10, 2010.)

Chapter 6

1. BrainyQuote, "Arnold H. Glasow Quotes" www.brainyquote.com/quotes/quotes/a/arnoldhgl105310.html (accessed August 10, 2010.)

Chapter 7

1. Robert Kiyosaki, *Rich Dad Poor Dad*. (New York: Business Plus, 1998)

Chapter 8

1. Quotes.net, "Herb Brody Quotes" http://www.quotes.net/authors/Herb+Brody (accessed August 10, 2010.

Chapter 9

1. Earl Nightingale, "Acres of Diamonds" www.nightingale.com/AE_Article~i~156~article~ACRESOFDIAMONDS.aspx (accessed August 12, 2010.)

Chapter 11

1. David, "Introvert Joke" introvertretreat.com/?p=67 (accessed August 12, 2010.)